AF574149

Making Model Soldiers

MICHAEL BLAKE

Making Model Soldiers

Stanley Paul, London

Stanley Paul & Co Ltd
3 Fitzroy Square, London W1P 6JD

An Imprint of the Hutchinson Publishing Group

London Melbourne Sydney Auckland
Wellington Johannesburg and agencies
throughout the world

First published 1975

Set in Monotype Plantin

Printed in Great Britain by
Flarepath Printers Ltd, St Albans, Hertfordshire
and bound by Wm Brendon & Son Ltd
of Tiptree, Essex

ISBN 0 09 124000 X

Contents

1 From Toy Soldier to Military Miniature

Warfare is as old as man, and it seems likely that model soldiers are almost as old as war. It is not the purpose of this volume to trace the history of toy and model soldiers, particularly as this has already been done in depth in other books, but a brief introduction to the history of the hobby may be of interest to newcomers. For those who would like to find out more some books on the subject are listed in the appendices.

One point which should perhaps be clarified at the start is that of basic terminology used in this book. No such simplification is possible outside its pages because collectors and enthusiasts all have their own idea of what the object of their attention should be called. I shall refer to the figures primarily made for collectors, whether the do-it-yourself type or not, as model soldiers or military miniatures. Those figures primarily made for the mass children's market will be referred to as toy soldiers. One of the purposes of this book will be to show you how you can make toy soldiers into model soldiers. However, this was not the evolutionary process referred to in the title of this chapter. The intention was to convey the gradual change in emphasis for both makers and collectors away from simple toy-like figures towards the modern super-detailed connoisseur figures.

The first primitive figures found in tombs and graves could well have been playthings or idols. The real history of toy and model soldiers as we know them today began in the eighteenth century, when the first mass-produced figures appeared in some numbers. These were flat figures, that is, they were virtually two-dimensional, not fully round. These figures are still very popular on the continent, and now we are members of the EEC perhaps we shall see more of these delightful and highly detailed pieces in this country. There were also paper and card figures but these are, even now, not really considered part of the hobby. The next stage in the story was the appearance of the round solid figure, again on the continent, some time around the end of the eighteenth century. These figures were given a further boost in the 1870s by the appearance of models with plug-in heads, made by the firm of Heyde in Germany. The next major change came, at last, from this country. In the 1890s, smart painted hollow cast figures made their debut, produced by the firm of William Britains Ltd, of London. The story of these soldier-makers supreme has been told elsewhere, but without a doubt these figures formed the basis of most British collections for the next seventy years, as well as providing many boys with hours of fun. They were, of course, marketed as toys, but it is quite possible that more were bought by boys in their second childhood than in their first. Following World War Two, however, a new kind of figure was introduced. These were still metal, but were no longer toys, and were much more expensive than Britains'. This was the beginning of the great increase in interest in the world of model soldiers, an interest which is still growing, with better and bigger figures appearing at a bewildering rate.

The next development was the appearance of the plastic figure, still not fully accepted in some model soldier circles. This reluctance to accept the 'steadfast plastic soldier' alongside his old established comrade the 'steadfast tin soldier' was understandable at first, when the figures produced were often crude and lacking in detail. Eventually, however, the newcomer has almost replaced the metal figure; indeed in the toy field metal figures have disappeared almost completely. The main reasons for this change are plastic's cheapness and the fine detailing which can be achieved. The development of the plastic model kit, principally by Airfix in this country, also heralded a new type of soldier in kit form. The first Airfix kits were rather simple, large scale historical figures, aimed at children. Historex then produced their beautifully detailed 54 mm kits of French troops of the Revolution and First Empire (c 1791–1815) in which every part which can be is a separate piece. Airfix then re-entered this field with a new series in 54 mm, on somewhat simpler lines than Historex, but of excellent quality. The popularity of these soldier kits has been increased by boys who have been brought up on plastic kits of cars, planes and ships, and who have created a generation who expect to construct the figure, and indeed enjoy doing so, before painting it.

The other change is a change in the attitude of the hobbyist rather than in the hobby. The old-style collector, because of the

54 mm Indian Army figure by Rose Miniatures, painted and photographed by the makers.

availability of masses of toy soldiers of the Britains' type, based his collection on these figures. This led to a parade ground type collection, going for mass effect rather than individual detail. The figures which made this type of collection possible are now worth many times their original value, and often more than modern collectors' figures. Thus, nowadays they are collected as antiques and investments rather than as model soldiers and potential conversion material. The figures available now, both metal and plastic, lend themselves to a more individual approach. This is a natural result of their cost, and of their individual detail, and has resulted in modern collectors building up collections based on displays, of individual figures or small groups, and dioramas, to ensure that the fineness of the models is seen to its best advantage.

Garrison (Greenwood and Ball) 25 mm Napoleonic wargames figures, painted by the makers, and showing the amount of detail which can be picked out even at this small scale. Photo by Humphrey-Saunders Studios Ltd.

54 mm sailors, to show that not all model soldiers are soldiers! Figures by Rose Miniatures, painted and photographed by the makers.

The other change has been in the collectors themselves. The wide variety of people who are model soldier enthusiasts has not altered, nor has the fact that some are only collectors in the sense that they buy and display finished figures, whilst others buy castings which they then animate and paint themselves. What has changed is that there are now many more of the latter who, though obtaining their enjoyment from the making and painting of models, want to be able to finish their figures accurately down to the last detail without being involved in deep research into military history. This has led to a great increase in the availability of published material on military dress, uniforms and equipment designed to meet this need. Some of the most useful of these are listed in the appendices. Many makers now provide a short cut for the modeller in the form of information sheets giving painting details, and sometimes some historical background, which are usually provided free with the figures when purchased. In some cases a photograph or line drawing of a finished figure is also included to help the modeller. Some metal figures are also sold in kit form, both to reduce the cost because the time spent in assembling and animating is saved, and because many modellers prefer to be able to put the figure together as they wish. The solid and kit models have been identified in the list of makers to help the reader choose whichever he prefers. The makers' catalogues and lists have also improved, often forming small magazines in their own right and containing useful information on painting techniques and uniform details. Unfortunately this has also led to an increase in the cost of such catalogues, but they usually represent good value for money.

2 Getting Started

The model soldier market is bewilderingly well stocked today, with figures of every nationality and in a wide range of scales available. Add to this the various materials in which models are made, mainly types of soft metal and plastic, and it is almost enough to daunt a beginner.

This chapter is devoted to leading the reader, a potential modeller, through the maze and helping him to decide where and with what to start. Let us begin with scales, and first of all explain just what is meant when one talks about the scale of a figure. As each model is a replica of a real-life soldier, the size of the model reflects the size of the original; thus if the man is 6 ft tall and the figure is 6 in tall, each 1 in on the figure represents 12 in on the man. Model scales have led the way with metrication, however, and are usually expressed in millimetres, for example a figure is spoken of as being 54 mm. This means that when measured the model soldier will be 54 mm in height representing an average soldier of 5 ft 8 in to 6 ft tall (or 9 mm to 1 ft). This scale, 54 mm, is then a proportional scale of 1 mm or inch (on the model) to 32 mm or inches (in real life), expressed as 1/32, and is in fact the most popular figure scale. Simple, you think? Unfortunately not, because makers have their own interpretations of just what measurements should be used. Britains Ltd used to explain their policy thus: 'We have taken a man 5 ft 8 in high standing erect and excluding headgear, reduced him to $2\frac{1}{8}$ in which is a reduction of 32:1 or a scale of $\frac{3}{8}$ in = 1 ft. This is constant scale to which all our models are made and is known as "standard size".' Other makers have taken different proportions, for example including the base or headgear, and so it is not always possible to mix figures which are supposed to be in the same scale. Sometimes this disparity can be a distinct advantage, however; when one is seeking to show differences in character between figures in a group, which can be emphasized by using figures of various makes and therefore proportions and heights, just as in life people do not come all exactly the same proportion. One area in which it is particularly important to watch this size difference is when using parts from various makers to convert a figure, because, for example, a head too large for a body can easily spoil an otherwise excellent model. So it pays to familiarize oneself with the sizes and proportions used by the various makers before attempting to combine what may be ill-matching parts.

Let us now take a look at the other main scales, starting with the smallest and working up. In Appendix 1 the scales produced by each maker are listed, together with comments on the figures themselves, so in this brief run-through I will do little more than mention the scales and give some general remarks on possible uses.

The smallest figures currently produced, and these must surely be the smallest a model soldier can be and still remain recognizable as such, are around 1/300, 1/285 and 1/200. Quite a large range of periods, including Ancient, Napoleonic, American Civil War and Modern (World War Two and later) are currently available. The various makers' ranges do not necessarily mix well, but at such small scales the differences are often minor enough to escape notice. These very small scale figures and equipment incorporate a surprising amount of detail. Their main use is by wargamers who want to fight large battles using a very small figure-to-man ratio (perhaps even one figure represents one man) or who wish to play on a small area. However, this does not mean that they are of no interest to a modeller or collector, because they paint up well and can be used for mass effect in dioramas of both action scenes and parade ground displays, again using a one-to-one figure-to-man or-weapon ratio. All the ranges produced at the moment are in metal, but are very reasonably priced and well within the reach of even the pocket-money collector in large numbers. One of the problems is that there are few sources of ready-made buildings or scenery in the market, but such pieces are quite easily made in such small scales, and Bellona are now producing such items.

The next scale is N gauge, a popular model railway scale, where N stands for 9 mm which is the track gauge. The actual scale varies but is 1/148 in Great Britain. This means that there are plenty of scale buildings, trees and other terrain pieces, etc., available from model railway hobby shops, so that the wargamer or modeller can concentrate on the figures themselves. The

Lasset (Greenwood and Ball) 54 mm Knights and Ancients, showing the matt grey primer/undercoat in which the figures are supplied. Photo by Humphrey-Saunders Studios Ltd.

infantry figures stand around ½ in (13 mm) tall, and are only produced by the American Jack Scruby, in metal, at the moment. However, the range covers Ancient, Eighteenth Century, Napoleonic, American Civil War and Colonial (1880–1918) periods and the scale is therefore well represented.

Next up the list is 15 mm, or 1/120 scale with 2½ mm representing 1 ft. All the main wargames periods are again available, and again the diorama maker can create some very effective scenes using these metal figures, either as they come or with extra detailing added. N gauge terrain pieces can again be used quite effectively both for wargaming and dioramas.

We have now reached the main wargames scales of HO/OO and 25 mm, where again the confusion is added to by different makers producing figures in these scales which are not in scale with each other's ranges. Taking HO/OO first, let us clarify just what this or rather these scales are in terms of measurements. HO is a scale of 3·5 mm to 1 ft or around 1/86; OO is a scale of 4 mm to 1 ft or 1/72, and was originally simply a British version of HO. In model soldier terms the height of the figure is used;

HO is usually referred to as 20 mm and OO as 25 mm. The biggest range of figures is produced by Airfix, who call their range of plastic small-scale figures HO/OO just to confuse the unwary, with forty-five sets of figures listed in the eleventh edition of their catalogue and new sets being added each year. Airfix themselves make railway buildings, castles and forts, and modern vehicles to the same scale, and of course the other ranges of buildings, etc., made for model railway layouts can be used. Miniature Figurines and Bellona also market ranges of plastic buildings and terrain pieces for these scales, which are intended for wargamers but can be used in dioramas to avoid having to scratch-build.

Before the appearance of wargames figures in HO/OO, the most popular size for wargaming was 30 mm or 1/60 scale, with 5 mm representing 1 ft. There are still a wide range of figures available in this scale, and it is my own particular favourite both for wargaming and for displays. To me, it combines the advantages of the larger scales, in that the figures are highly detailed individuals, with the advantages of smaller scales, in that quite large numbers of figures do not take up too great an amount of space. Unfortunately, there are no commercial buildings available in this scale so such pieces have to be scratch-built, and the range of equipment, i.e. artillery, weapons, etc., is very limited. Indeed, for some figures it is impossible to obtain the appropriate pieces and so again scratch-building is necessary. Figures are available in both metal and plastic, and most ranges will intermix satisfactorily.

There are next a number of intermediate scales around 35 mm (1/52 scale, 6 mm to 1 ft) to 40 mm (1/48 scale, 7 mm to 1 ft), mainly made to go with modern armour plastic kits by Japanese makers, except for the hand-painted Elastolin range by Hausser.

As we have already discussed 54 mm, the next scales are 75 mm and 77 mm. These are very close together, both being more or less 1/24 scale or 13 mm to 1 ft. At this scale, of course, the detailing has to be very good indeed, and equally the painting has to be of the same standard to pass muster. Because of their size, these figures are probably at their best displayed singly with, at most, a simple scenic base. This is also true of the 90 mm figures now more widely available, their scale being 1/20 or 15 mm to 1 ft. Both these sizes are in metal, but there are even larger figures in plastic kit form at 1/12 scale made by Airfix and

Aurora, and even 1/6 scale ball-jointed Action Man figures, with cloth uniforms and accurate scale plastic weapons and accessories, by Palitoy.

Having run rather rapidly through the various major scales available, perhaps we should consider briefly the two main materials used in the manufacture of military miniatures; plastic and metal. From the modeller's point of view, plastic is undoubtedly the most interesting because it is more easily workable and therefore convertible. There are, however, different types of plastic in use, and these do require different approaches in handling as explained in more detail in subsequent chapters. In addition, the various plastic kits have the added attraction of the assembly stages, and the modeller can enjoy this challenge almost as much as putting in the finishing touches. Painting can be carried out as the various parts are assembled, left until the figure is complete, or even some whilst the kit is still completely in pieces. Most metal figures come ready assembled, animated and primed, ready for painting, and the modeller has a major task ahead of him if he wishes to make any extensive alterations to the figure. It is possible to do so of course, and again the various techniques are discussed in detail later on.

So, having read this far, what is the next step for you now you have decided you would like to give it a try? Well, the first thing to do is to go along to your local model shop and take a look at the figures on sale there. If the salesman will cooperate, and as they are often modellers themselves they usually will, take a close look at the figures, handle them, examine the detail. Then, buy some of the makers' lists and catalogues, and one or all of the hobby magazines, and take them home to study at your leisure. If you do not happen to have a local stockist of military miniatures you will have to start by doing this, of course. It may well be that you have some basic ideas for your approach to the wonderful world of military miniatures; perhaps a picture you have seen, or a regiment with family or local connections, or just a uniform which appeals to you. In that case, search the lists for the figure you want. Some collectors approach the whole question of their collection rather like a military operation in itself, planning exactly what is to be represented down to the last detail. Others are impulse buyers who simply snap up the latest release in their favourite scale, or by their favourite maker, or just because it catches their eye in the shop. Somewhere in between are probably the majority of us, who have a theme for our proposed collection but who still cannot resist temptation when an occasional new model or scale comes along and takes our fancy. Whatever your approach, a great deal of pleasure can be obtained just from looking at, and drooling over, the makers' catalogues, trying to decide what to buy next.

3 Tools and Accessories

Opinions on what constitutes a basic toolkit differ widely. One modeller friend of mine is able to work wonders on cheap plastic toy soldiers with an old razor blade, balsa cement, toilet tissue and plasticene! Personally, I prefer something a little more sophisticated, but even my favourite implements might be considered inadequate by some. What I will suggest is a basic kit which will enable a modeller to clean up, assemble and paint model soldiers of any material, and also carry out most of the conversions detailed later in the book.

Basic Equipment

Craft knife and blades. There are many types – Swan-Morton, Humbrol, Xacto – and all will serve well. A new blade should always be used when trimming soft, polythene plastics to ensure a clean cut, but old blades should be retained and used on progressively tougher jobs, finally being reserved for cleaning up metal figures. If you can stretch the funds to two holders, one can be clearly identified with ink or paint and reserved for new blades. This avoids the danger of picking up the knife with a new blade in it and blunting the edge by scraping flash from a metal casting. A wide selection of blades is available, and one or two of each can be useful when trying to clean up a tricky corner which can only be reached with one type. They can be easily changed as the need arises. Costs vary; go for the cheapest you can find.

Needle and rat-tail files. These are the next most useful items. They come in various sizes, sections and grades of teeth, and although they are rather expensive a small selection is worth the investment. I would rate a fine-toothed, round, tapered file the most useful, with perhaps a knife-edged fine and a coarser triangular section next on the list. Handles are not necessary, indeed they only tend to get in the way. Costs range from 30p to 70p.

SELECTION OF TOOLS FROM BASIC TOOL KIT

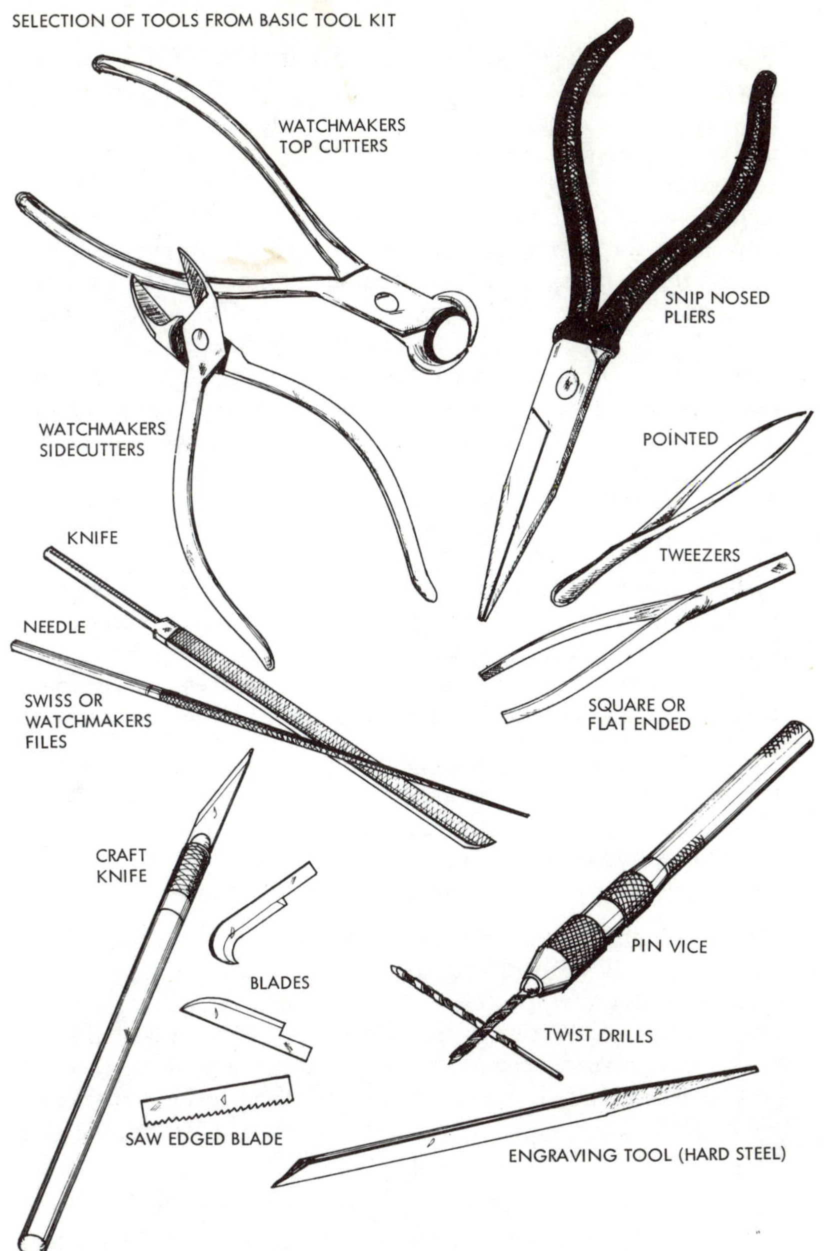

Watchmakers' sidecutters. These are likely to be of more use to wargamers or modellers in the smaller scales, where each figure may have a sprue and linking pieces to help the metal run right into every part, but they can also speed up removal of unwanted equipment, etc. Make sure they are the type which cut right up to one side of the blades. Watchmakers' topcutters are not quite so versatile for getting into corners, but a small pair of sidecutters backed up by a larger pair of topcutters will handle almost every problem. Box-joint construction is preferable to cross-joint because it is much stronger. These cutters can be used on wire such as piano wire, providing it is not too heavy a gauge, and are excellent for de-heading pins, but do watch out for flying pin heads! When cutting a pin or small length of wire, hold the longest piece in the fingers or with a pair of pliers, and the short piece in a vice or lump of plasticene to avoid it shooting off and into an eye. Costs vary from 50p upwards, so shop around.

Pliers. These are the smallest variety, either snipe-nosed or round-nosed being the best. Snipe-nosed hold small pieces to be bent, cut or pushed into plastic figures. Round-nosed can do all these, if rather less satisfactorily, but are excellent for bending curves or rings in wire. Prices are again around the 50p mark.

Tweezers. Again two pairs if possible (though one can always be borrowed from wife, girlfriend or sister); pointed end and blunt end. These are used to position small bits when gluing or painting, or holding additions like paper straps in place whilst they are stuck in position. Costs are minimal, from as little as 10p.

Pin vice. This is one of the most used items in my toolkit. The smallest size is probably the best, because a tight grip on the smallest drill you will want to use is needed. The pin vice works rather like a clutch pencil, but with a threaded action, and can hold a pin or sharp spike to punch holes, wire to be worked on (cut, sharpened) and, most useful of all, small drills for making holes in plastic or metal. This can be an expensive item, but you should be able to find one for less than £1.

Drills. The smallest sizes you can find, preferably with a couple of spares because, being so small, they can be all too easily broken. Another essential is something to keep them in; an empty plastic ballpen refill container is ideal. Prices range from a few pence to 50p.

Razor saw. A saw-edged blade which can be fitted into the craft knife will suffice, though for heavier jobs a proper razor saw will be needed. Blades are a few pence each, a saw around 50p.

Files. Other than the needle-files mentioned already, a larger and coarser file is very handy for cleaning up bases which, if cast with the figure, often have uneven lower surfaces. Abrafiles, which come in various grades, can be obtained from specialist D-I-Y shops.

Other small items. A few sheets of fine emery and sandpaper can come in useful. Graving tools or scribers can be used in place of blunt blades to add or strengthen joins and crease details, etc. Also useful are piano wire and fuse wire in different gauges, and pins of as many various sizes as possible, so never throw a pin away.

The total cost of the basic tools is only £2–3 even if they are all bought at the same time, but once purchased they will last the average modeller his lifetime. Other items will, of course, need constant replacement, but this can often be done at little cost because such small quantities are involved.

There are two other pieces of equipment which can be added to this kit to allow more complicated operations to be carried out, or to make things easier. One is a small electric soldering iron, and the other is a pyrogravure. The first is used with metal figures, and in skilled hands can be used to add and remove details. The pyrogravure is supplied by Historex, is used on plastic in a similar way to the soldering iron, and can also be used in animation to bend or straighten arms and legs. Both these items are quite expensive, however, and do require skilful use.

Adhesives and Modelling Materials

Adhesives. A number of different glues and adhesives will be required. The obvious ones are polystyrene (in tube and bottle, e.g. Mek-Pak) and balsa cement. For metal, a fast-acting epoxy such as Power-Pack, Devcon, etc., is essential. For gluing and filling in one operation, Plastic Padding and Araldite can be used but do take longer to set. A general purpose adhesive like UHU, Evostik or Bostik, and a PVA-type like Unibond, Clam, etc. are also useful. The latest glues on the market are the 'instant and permanent' types like Permabond, Devcon Zip Grip etc. which,

Selection of modelling items – plastic kit parts, Airfix on sprue, Historex partially assembled, craft knife, watchmakers sidecutters, snipenosed pliers, brushes, paints in tinlets and bottles, cocktail stick paint stirrers, and 'Humbrol' flatting agent for ensuring paint has a matt finish.

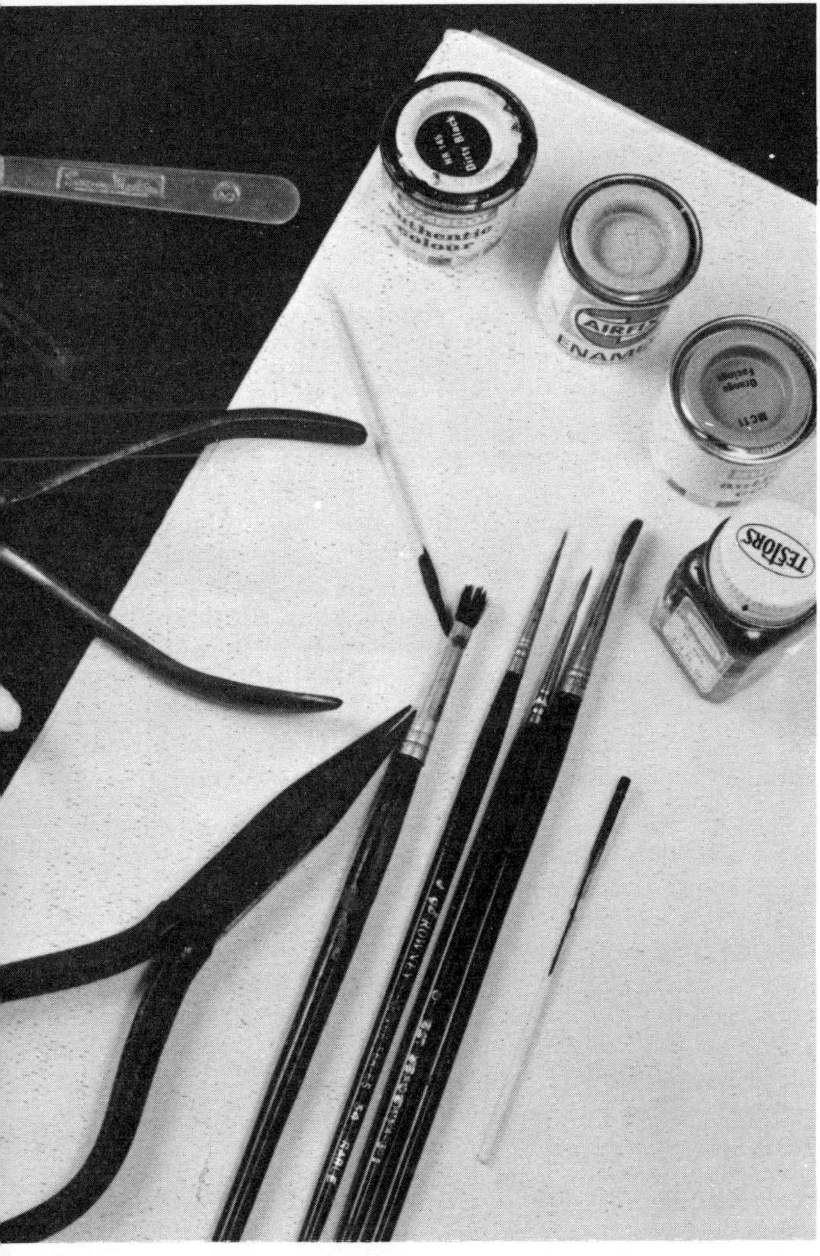
Dirty Black
TESTORS
ROWNEY

whilst excellent glues, must be used with great caution if sticking finger to finger is to be avoided!

Basic materials. There are various other materials which are all part of a military modeller's armament. Always keep close to hand some sheets of white paper in various thicknesses, some card, plastic card sheets and strips, and a box of tissues or a toilet roll. A steel ruler and, perhaps, a small set-square, with a rectangle of hardboard to rest upon, will make accurate cutting easy. A bulldog clip to hold down the paper or card being cut leaves both hands free. A packet of wooden and plastic cocktail sticks can be used both as tools and as materials.

Fillers. Figures often have gaps or holes which need filling, and there are a number of brands of plastic filler available. Plastic Padding has already been mentioned; this is mixed like an epoxy glue, i.e. from two tubes. Also available is an epoxy putty (such as Milliput) which comes as two blocks of putty rather like plasticene; when combined in equal proportions these make a filler which sets like metal (as does Plastic Padding) but which can be worked and applied like modelling clay or plasticene. Plastic fillers are available in single tubes, such as Humbrol's Body Putty, but the most useful and inexpensive type is Fine Grain Polyfilla. This is really intended for d-i-yourself activities but is excellent for modelling because it sets quickly without shrinking and is very hard and smooth.

Plasticene. For actually adding details or equipment, plasticene is my favourite. Indeed there is a diorama in the BMSS National Collection at Dodington House which has figures and equipment made entirely of plasticene. Because plasticene does not set hard, however, it must be treated to give it a tough skin. A coating of aero-modellers banana oil or ladies nail varnish will do the trick, though a second coat, or an application of PVA adhesive, is recommended before priming and painting. There are also modelling putties such as Plastone, Barbola and Das which do set hard, and a trial will quickly establish which you prefer to work with.

Additional materials. Wooden spills and a selection of balsa and obeche wood in sheets, rods and dowels will come in handy for adding touches like fences and other wooden bits to scenes and dioramas. Pipe cleaners are useful for plumes and tufts. Cotton, thread, twine and thin string can all be used for cords and ropes, either in their natural colours or suitably painted. Pins I have mentioned, but needles of various lengths and thicknesses can also be used as lances, colour staffs, etc.

Paints and Brushes

The next major items which need discussion are paints and brushes. Again there are divergent views on which are the best and which techniques achieve the best results. In this chapter we shall only look at the paints and brushes themselves, leaving painting for a later section. The old Britains and other toy soldiers were painted in bright prime colours with a shiny gloss finish. Many collectors continue this approach with conversions or figures they repaint. Gloss paint is still used by some Britains collectors, and by some wargamers for their wargames armies, because of its high resistance to handling. However, for the majority of military miniatures including repainted toys and wargames figures matt finish is used, with gloss and semi-gloss for items which have a natural shine or sheen such as polished boots and brushed horses.

Good quality brushes are essential, and a sound investment. It is impossible to over-emphasize this, because even the best quality casting will be ruined if the paint is applied with a brush resembling those used to paint walls. At one time the right quality brushes could only be bought from artists' suppliers, and were usually Winsor and Newton, or Rowney's water-colour brushes. The choice is now much wider, with many suppliers and makers producing their own brushes, and many model shops stocking good quality brushes where before they only had splay-ended glue-daubers. Buy the best sable you can afford in one of the ranges available to you. If you have to buy by post, both the Historex and Seagull ranges are excellent, varying in price from 26p for size 000 to 93p for size 6.

A word about brush sizes. The usual sizes run from 1, the smallest, to 6, the largest you are likely to be able to use on a figure. The sizes below 1 are numbered with zeros, and the more zeros the smaller the brush. Whilst 00000 are available, for all practical purposes an 000 is as small as you are likely to need even for the finest detail. In fact, what counts is not so much the size of the brush as the sharpness of the point, and this is where the high quality brushes score. They have a finer point and keep it longer, and therefore a good sable no. 3, which holds plenty of paint, can be used to paint fine details. Practice does make perfect, of course, and when you begin you may prefer to have some very small, say 00 and 000, brushes to tackle the finer details, but as you gain confidence and expertise you will find you can usually paint everything with a 1 or 2 without difficulty. However as a basic set I would suggest one each of nos. 000, 00, 1, and 3 pointed, with perhaps a no. 2 or 3 spade-ended.

Having invested in a good set of brushes, they must be looked after. It is best to adopt a routine which will keep them, and your paints, in good condition. When mixing, never lift paint from pots or jars with the brush, use your lid opener or stirrer. When you are changing colours, always clean the brush in two jars of turps or white spirit. Wash the brush in the first jar, which will quickly become dirty, then mop the turps from the bristles on a pad of clean cloth or paper tissue resting on your work surface, drawing the brush gently across the surface to retain the point. Then rinse the brush in the second pot of turps, which should stay reasonably clean, and again mop the surplus on to the cloth or tissue. This procedure should also be followed when you have finished painting, but is completed by washing the brush in warm, soapy water. The soap should be left in the bristles, the point shaped on the palm of the hand, and the brush put away until required again. The soap is rinsed out before use next time. With care a good brush will last for months even with almost constant use on metal figures, which do tend to wear the point more quickly than plastic.

We have now come to the paints themselves, and once again the choice is wide and opinions on the best types vary almost from modeller to modeller. I will take a look at the main types and ranges readily available and make a few suggestions for beginners. Old hands, and newcomers as they gain experience, will have their own opinions and preferences, but perhaps some of the information here will encourage them to try something new with surprising results. To a large extent, the paints used will depend on the overall effect desired. Gloss paints which are used to give a very toy-like appearance to figures have already been mentioned. Lynn Sangster, writing in the Historex catalogue, says that he aims for a slight sheen or eggshell finish on his Historex figures, which he achieves using combinations of Historex oil-based poster paint, Humbrol Railway enamels, and artists' oil paints. Personally I like a very matt finish, with a sheen (not a shine) only on polished or varnished items, and I use a wide assortment of oil-based enamels such as Testor, Airfix and Humbrol, and water-based acrylics like Plaka and Rowney's Designers Gouache. Eddie Jones, again in the Historex catalogue, explains his efforts to find a means of achieving different textures for the various materials which make up a uniform, and says that he has been able to achieve this effect by mixing Rowney's Flow Formula Cryla paint with their Acrylic Designers' Gouache to obtain surfaces from the matt of cloth to the sheen of animal skin.

However, let us now take a look at the makers and types in detail. Humbrol now produce what is undoubtedly the largest range of oil-based enamels. They have three ranges, Enamels in gloss and matt, Railway enamels in matt and semi gloss, and Authentics in all three finishes, all in 15 ml tinlets. They cover many different shades, and are clearly identified as to the colour they represent. The Authentics range is, in fact, broken down into groups of colours which are sold as sets as well as singly (such as USAF, RAF, Ceremonial Uniforms, Napoleonics, etc.) with each colour identified with the original source, for example in the French Prussian Napoleonic set there are dragoon green, French blue, sky blue, Polish crimson, orange facings and Prussian dragoon blue.

Airfix produce a very useful range of eighteen gloss and twenty-seven matt enamels, again in tinlets, which provide most of the military colours required by the modeller. The colours are listed in their catalogue. Both makers also have matt and gloss varnish and thinners.

The US firm of Testors now market their small jars of paints in this country, and the range includes some excellent shades not available in Humbrol or Airfix, in particular a bright flat sky blue which puts other sky blues to shame. Another range of matt and gloss paints are produced as Pactra'namel, but the basis of these paints is highly poisonous, and as the enamel is also flammable they are probably best left alone. In any case I have tried them, and I was not very impressed with the results.

Humbrol also have a range of spray paints, but these are all gloss finish. For matt sprays, U-Spray have white, black, white primer and varnish. The Dupli-color car spray paints have some useful shades including a matt grey primer.

Artists' oils are also oil-based of course, and there are a number of ranges readily available from art supply shops. Most modellers who use these paints recommend the best quality available, but Dick Higgs of Miniature Figurines uses Student oil colours, and recommends them. Artists' oils can easily be mixed with the other oil-based paints already mentioned to achieve just the right shade, but more of this later. Poster colours can be oil-or water-based. Of the former type, Campaign Colours have a range of thirty-two uniform colours and five horse colours, and are recommended by The Old Guard. This paint dries very slowly to allow shading to a very flat finish, and whilst my own painting attempts with these paints have not been very successful, I have seen them used to great effect by other modellers. Certainly in terms of quantity they represent very good value, as they come in large jars. Also oil-bound is the small range of paints marketed by Historex Agents.

Moving on to the water-based paints, my own favourite is the Pelikan Plaka range. These are very quick drying, to a tough matt finish, and are opaque if used slightly thinned, or can be used as a translucent wash if thinned sufficiently. The colours are very clear and bright, and are particularly good for gaudy full-dress uniforms. Large art shops usually have Pelikan paints, or they can be obtained by post from Mainly Military. Both Winsor and Newton and Rowney have designers' gouache ranges, and many modellers paint exclusively with these paints. A very wide colour range is available, and all are intermixable. A comparatively recent development by Rowney is their Acrylic Designers' Gouache, which has the combined advantages of being water-based and yet waterproof when dry. These gouaches come in small tubes, but there are also cheaper acrylic paints available in large tubes, such as Rowney PVA, and the newer Flow Formula Cryla. All these types are available from art shops and the like. Rose Miniatures produce their own small range of water-based casein colours, and these can be obtained by post.

All of the ranges and types mentioned include metal colours. In some this is simply gold and silver. Humbrol also have brass, copper, steel, silver plate and gunmetal. These are very good paints, and are useful no matter what other type of paint is used. Testor gold is particularly good as it is very fine grained, and gives a smooth, metallic-looking finish which is better than most other golds, which usually have a very coarse texture.

Finally, what colours will be needed to paint your military miniatures? In fact surprisingly few, because paints with the same base are intermixable and so any shade or colour can be mixed as required. However, if you are painting large numbers of figures for a wargames army or diorama, it is better to use ready mixed colours to ensure that, if you use up all your supply of one shade, the next batch will be exactly the same. Starting from scratch with oil-based enamels, both Humbrol or Airfix ranges or ordinary matt colours cover all the usual uniform colours. In gloss you will need only black, gold, silver, copper, bronze, gunmetal and silver plate. The Humbrol Railway browns are useful for horse colours. The complete Airfix range in matt, or similar colours in Humbrol, will give you a comprehensive choice, and will enable you to paint most figures using colours straight from the tin. The more unusual colours, and other shades of the basic range, can then be added as the need arises. If funds are limited, the initial selection can be reduced to the basic colours needed for the uniforms you intend to start with. For example; if you are going to paint American Civil War figures, a basic selection might consist of dark blue, light blue, light grey, white, black, dark brown, buff, red, yellow, green and flesh. For more colourful periods a larger number of colours would be needed. If the figures to be painted are larger collectors' pieces then a smaller palette of colours can be used, because intermediate shades will be mixed as required. In the water-based paints, a basic uniform palette suggested by Eddie Jones in the Historex catalogue would be middle yellow, yellow ochre, cadmium red, scarlet, crimson, burnt sienna, sky blue, ultramarine, Prussian blue, deep green, black and white. In Plaka, the selection of sixteen colours listed by Mainly Military will meet most needs. These are flesh, red-violet, red-brown, yellow, carmine, deep blue, brown, orange, vermilion, turquoise blue, yellow ochre, deep madder, green, grey, black and white. The Historex oil-bound poster paint range consists of only eight colours – black, dark blue, light blue, lemon yellow, yellow ochre, red, crimson and green – and with the addition of a white oil-based enamel (Humbrol or Airfix) would again comprise a good selection for uniform colours.

With all our tools and our paints ready, and gleaming model soldiers waiting to be brought to life as we clean them and then clothe them in their uniforms, we lack only one essential before we can start. Somewhere to work. Undoubtedly the ideal work top is an old-fashioned roll-topped desk, because the roller top can be closed down over our efforts to give a neat and tidy appearance to any casual examination. Unfortunately few of us have such a desk, and many must make do with a tray and the kitchen table top on loan for the evening. This need be no hindrance. The essential requirements are a steady surface such as a table or desk, and a tray or pad to protect it. A clear area, with the various items you will need laid out around it, will enable you to work on your figures without the frustration of constantly mislaying the needle-file or copper wire. A compartmented tray, like the kind used for cutlery or photographic slides, is useful for keeping the numerous small tools, and the smaller bits and pieces listed in the basic tool and equipment list. Paints are best kept in similar trays or shallow boxes, and grouped by colours. Thus all the browns would go in one box, greens in another and so on. Brushes can be kept the same way, or stood upright, on the ends of their handles to protect their bristles, in jars or mugs.

The 'bits box' is an indispensable part of any military modellers' armoury. In fact it is usually a number of boxes, all with different kinds of bits. Some are readily identified as parts (or potential parts) of models, such as weapons, heads, arms, etc. Other bits are less easily given definite purposes; items such as empty ball pens, refills, fancy bottle tops, small pieces of broken dress jewellery, and the like. These are the things which will come in useful one day, and are kept because a modellers' motto is NTAA – Never Throw Anything Away! To keep all these assorted bits in some semblance of order, so that certain items such as heads, or swords, can be found, and the right one selected reasonably quickly, the bits box needs to be made up of a number of small drawers. The plastic or metal cabinets with transparent plastic pull-out drawers are ideal. These can be bought quite cheaply from Woolworths or tool shops. Another kind of box which is useful for keeping small pieces in is the fishing tackle box, which has a hinged upper tray which lifts up and back when the box is opened. Again most Woolworths carry a good, cheap selection.

One final suggestion which male readers may find surprising. When you are working on models, whether cleaning them up, casting, painting or whatever, wear an apron. This will protect your clothes and save you having to change your trousers whenever you want to model, and it will catch all the tiddly bits which you drop into your lap. This is particularly important if you happen to be filing metal castings in the living room over a brand new carpet!

4 Painting Techniques

Painting can transform a mediocre figure into a collector's piece, but it can also turn a connoisseur's figure into a toy soldier. So having bought your first figure, how do you go about painting it to bring out the best? The actual technique will depend both on the size of the figure, and on the paints you intend to use. Let us first run through the simpler approach for wargames or diorama figures, in small scales but large numbers, and then move on to more sophisticated techniques for the true military miniature.

The basic requirement for any figure, metal or plastic, is a smooth, sound and light-coloured surface for the paint. Metal soldiers can fall victim to chemical breakdowns on their surfaces which result in the deterioration of the paint, and the figure is ruined. Theories as to what causes this reaction abound, the blame being laid variously on the lead content, the tin content, the temperature and the moisture content of the atmosphere. Whatever the cause, the effect is horrible, and to avoid this happening to your figures the best treatment is to ensure the metal is well primed. With small figures this is most easily done with a spray paint such as U-Spray white primer, or with a primer applied with an air-brush. The finer detail on a larger collectors' piece deserves rather more careful treatment, and a primer is best applied with a brush. Ordinary household metal primer, thinned with turps and applied carefully in a wash all over the figure, will suffice. Bryan Holding, BMSS Bristol, recommends a mixture of one part matt white and one part matt Humbrol polyurethane varnish to three parts turps. This mixture can be prepared in bulk and kept ready-mixed for application as required. Many assembled metal figures come ready primed and so do not need a further coat of primer.

This priming coat, whether makers' or modellers', will achieve the smooth and sound surface required and, if a white or yellow primer has been used, also provides the light background mentioned before as a basic requirement. However, some makers prime with a grey primer, and there are car-colour sprays with grey primers. If either of these have been used, then another very thin coat of white will help to bring out the true colours of the paints. This second coat can be any matt white paint, even white household emulsion thinned to flow easily and evenly over the figure without obscuring detail. Two or more thin coats of primer or white undercoat are better than one thick coat, because fine detail can often be obscured. Having primed and undercoated, leave the figure for as long as possible to dry really hard before painting. Indeed, U-Spray white primer or matt white can still tend to lift under certain colours, even when left to dry for forty-eight hours or more, and an application of a matt spray varnish such as Testors' Dullcoate is advisable to seal the surface permanently before painting.

So far we have only mentioned metal figures. The same need for a good, light-coloured surface applies to plastic, but because most plastic figures are in a white or creamy-white plastic there is no need to prime and undercoat. However, if the figures to be painted are polythene, such as the Airfix 1/32 series, surface adhesion can be a problem. This is also true of conversions, where a figure may have a variety of materials added, in a variety of colours. The best way to seal off all these surfaces, and to provide a good key for a white undercoat, is to apply a coat of PVA adhesive such as Clam or Unibond. These glues are useful in any modeller's tool kit because they are also excellent though slow-acting adhesives. The PVA will form a hard skin over the figure, but will pull in tight when dry and so can be applied reasonably liberally. PVA is a cream-like white substance, and to assist with the application over a figure that may well be thoroughly greasy from extensive handling, pour some of the adhesive into a screw-top jar, and mix in a few drops of washing-up liquid. This will act as a wetting agent and ensure that the PVA will cover greasy areas without difficulty. The glue may still be a little thick and can be thinned with water to obtain the right flow. The original tin or tub of PVA can now still be used where a thick glue is needed. Though white in the jar, PVA dries transparent, and so a thin white undercoat is still required. I have experimented with mixing matt white water-based paint with the PVA and this does work.

The row of shiny castings has now been transformed into a row of dull white figures and we are ready to bring them to life.

With your work area laid out as described in the previous chapter, everything will be ready at hand. To assist in handling the figures whilst they are being painted, they can be temporarily stuck to small blocks of wood, although I find that metal figures can be handled by the base and bayonet until the latter is painted, and the base then painted after the bayonet has dried.

Whether metal or plastic, the approach is the same. The first step is to put on the colour which covers the largest area. This is usually the coat or jacket, and the paint should be flowed on from a heavily loaded brush with no attempt to keep to the area of the coat alone; indeed it is essential that the paint goes onto other adjoining areas such as trousers. In effect, the whole top half of the figure including hands and musket is liberally covered in the coat colour. Avoid brushing, that is working the paint with the brush. The paint should be applied by allowing it to flow onto the figure from the edge of the brush. Do not worry if the paint collects under arms and in creases. The formula of the new enamels ensures that the paint will dry out to a thin film even if applied quite thickly. All the figures to be painted have the one colour applied, making sure that no little spots are missed, particularly under arms. You may be wondering why I have suddenly advocated what seem to be such slap-dash methods after all the careful preparation. You will see why when we move on to the next stage. The paint should be allowed to dry, and this will take around twenty-four hours. For this reason I always paint a number of different units at the same time, so that there are groups of figures which have had the main uniform colour painted and are dry. These are then ready for the next colour when another unit or two have had their basic colour painted.

Let us look at a particular figure as an example, and work through the next steps one by one. Let us take an Airfix HO/OO Waterloo British infantryman as the figure, and illustration number 257 in P. Kannik's book *Military Uniforms of the World* as our painting guide. The uniform is that of an infantryman of the King's German Legion 1812. The figures will already have their red coats painted. The next item to paint is their grey overalls. The technique is the same as for the coat except that, where the overall top meets the jacket, the paint is applied carefully. Because the red will have extended down onto the top of the trousers, there can be no problem with the two colours meeting and hiding all the plastic, and this, of course, is the

A. Red coat only - note overlap onto other areas.
B. Grey overalls and all black items now painted - overlapped onto unpainted areas but carefully painted up to borders with red coat.
C. Brown musket and all white areas.

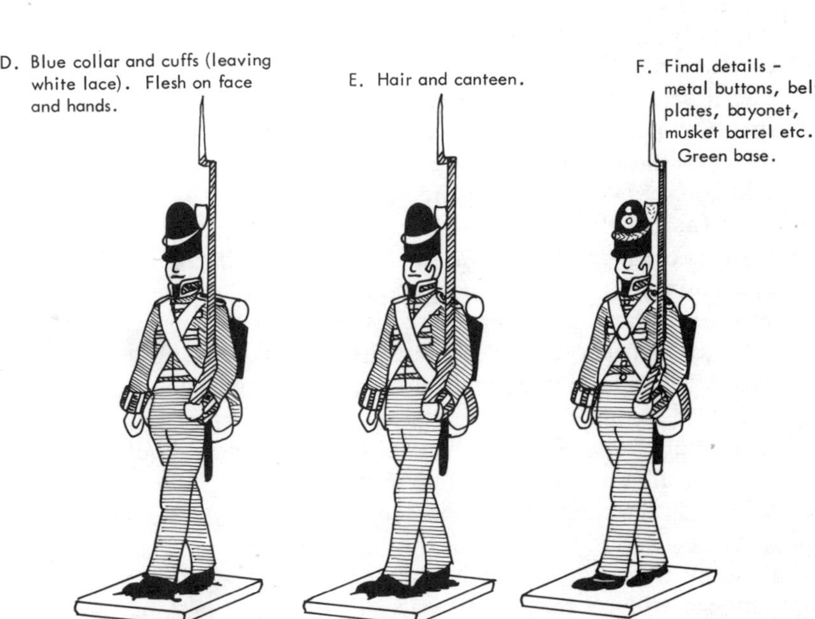
D. Blue collar and cuffs (leaving white lace). Flesh on face and hands.
E. Hair and canteen.
F. Final details - metal buttons, belt plates, bayonet, musket barrel etc. Green base.

reason for making sure that the paint from the item being painted goes well over onto any adjoining item not yet painted. With all the overalls painted, the next colour can be applied. This is black for shako, stock, bayonet scabbard, boots, gaiters, cartridge box, and knapsack. The musket can be painted brown now. Next comes white, which means the lacing across the coat front, cross-belts and straps, the haversack, shako plume and cords, collar and shoulder straps. The reason for painting the collar and shoulder strap white is that it is far easier then to paint in the blue, leaving a thin white edging, than to try to paint such a fine line in white around the blue. Again care is taken where the white is over an area already painted, but elsewhere the white is allowed to spread onto bare plastic. The cuffs and lace can be painted in the same way, or the blue painted first and then the white lace. This second dip in the white paint can be useful for painting in any items missed first time around. In fact, blue is the next colour to be applied. Follow this with the face and hands, then hair, light blue for the canteen, and the metal items such as the shako plate, bayonet and musket barrel. Finish with a bright green base to set all the other colours off, and the result should be a work of art!

The great advantage of this overlap approach is that it avoids unsightly gaps between colours, which so often result from carefully painting each colour to the edge of the area, only to find that it was not quite to the edge after all. It also helps to ensure that the paint is applied liberally enough to really cover the metal or plastic, because care is only needed in parts. As I have said before, avoid working the brush. The paint should just flow from the bristles onto the figure. If it does not, it is too thick. Paint is often too thick if used straight from the tin for painting such things as straps or frogging, so thin it to the right consistency with turps. It is better to apply the colour in two separate attempts to cover the base colour than to make fine lining difficult with a thick paint which will not run off the brush.

I have assumed that the figures are allowed to dry between each application of colour, but with practice you should be able to paint all the colours at one sitting providing the main body colour is dry. However, this does require care if the colour underneath is not to bleed through the later application, particularly if the top colour is lighter. I would suggest that a little patience will be rewarded, especially at the beginning. Indeed, the example chosen is rather a complicated uniform, and Airfix figures are rather small. When first attempting to paint, it is as well to stick to the basic colours, leaving refinements such as the white lace until you have greater confidence in your ability. The old cliché 'practice makes perfect' is almost right in the case of painting, but for most of us it is only that 'practice makes better'. I can still remember my delight as I proudly showed my wife the Airfix American Civil War artillerymen I had actually managed to give red collars, and that was months after I had started painting wargames figures. Some people do have a feel for painting, and for them it comes that much easier. To those who find painting difficult, I suggest that they persevere with the methods described, and with time they will be able to tackle even the finest detail.

There are some problems which daunt most modellers when they first try painting military miniatures, whether small- or large-scale figures. One is that of tartans. Highlanders are available in all sizes, and have a great appeal to almost everyone. With the smaller scales, particularly for wargames, a simplified approach can overcome the terror of tartans and enable even a beginner to add a regiment of hairy highlanders to his collection. Most military tartans are based on the set or pattern known as the 'military set' which was first worn by the 42nd Highlanders (Black Watch). The first step is to paint the whole kilt dark blue. Over this, black horizontal and vertical lines are painted to form the dark blue into squares. The whole effect is then lightened by the addition of dark green lines on the black, to make the black become just a fine edging to the green. This is really enough for wargames figures, but the larger scales require a rather more detailed approach. Additional fine black lines are now added linking the blue squares, and also running through the centre of both green and blue. Careful examination of most other tartans will enable them to be broken down into their components and painted in the same way. A. H. Bowling's book *Scottish Regiments and Uniforms* 1660–1914 is useful in this respect because the small colour illustrations show the overall effect of the various tartans when reduced in size.

Another problem which vexes modellers is that of flags. Again the problem can be tackled in two ways, depending on the scale of the figures for which a colour or standard is required. Most Airfix sets include a colour bearer, but the colour is rarely of the correct size. Metal makers usually only provide a pole. The flag itself can be made from a number of different materials. Personally I use paper for wargames flags because, if they are to look at their most effective, they need to be carried well stiffened in the breeze. This is necessarily rather artificial, of course, because the heavy silk would normally hang and drape around the staff except in a really high wind, but this does rather lose the effect of a nicely painted colour waving above the unit as it charges at the enemy. Alternatively, metal kitchen foil or thin sheet metal can be used, or any of the other materials described later for the larger scales.

The approach I use begins with the cutting out of the correct size for the flag from a good quality white paper, which when folded and stuck will be the right thickness. The sleeve of material which attaches to the staff must be allowed for when measuring the width. The amount needed will depend on the thickness of the staff, which is best made from something like piano wire. If the figure has a pole with a head decoration, such as an eagle or crown, but the pole itself is too thick in scale, the decorations can be cut from the over-size pole, drilled, and stuck on to a new piano wire staff. The old staff is carefully cut from the figure and the hands drilled to allow the piano wire to be pushed through and glued in place.

Having cut the flag to the right size and shape it is stuck on to the staff. If the flag is mainly a background colour with a design upon it, such as British regimental colours, the next step is to paint the whole flag the background colour. If the right colour paper is available then this could be used. When the background is dry, the design is sketched on it in soft pencil. It can help if a few practice attempts at reducing the design to the correct size and proportions are made first on plain paper. When the design is correct, and this may take a little time, ink in the correct lines with a draughtsman's pen and erase the pencil with a very soft rubber. The design can now be painted, and here quick drying paints such as gouache are best so that the whole design can be painted at one sitting. Where gold or silver embroidery is used in the original, the corresponding parts of the design should be painted with yellow or pale grey as an undercoat to the metallic colour. If the flag is a more complicated design without a predominant background colour, such as British Kings' colours, the design is sketched in pencil, and inked in, on the plain white paper, and then painted. When the whole flag has been painted, the outline of the design is again inked in to give greater definition, and this is the final touch which finishes the whole effect. If there is a fringe to the colour, this can be cut with a sharp knife, then painted the appropriate colour.

The same method and material can be used for flags for larger scale figures, but the best results are obtained with a rather different approach. The flag itself can be made from paper, but it is difficult to achieve realistic draping. A fine-weave linen handkerchief can be used, with the fringe made by pulling out some threads. Some paints will not work well on the linen, but the new fabric paints now available are ideal of course. Tracing linen is another suitable material, but the stiffening must be washed out first. The flag can then be painted as already described. With either of these linens the flag can be draped and left to hang naturally or, when the required hang has been formed, the whole flag can be coated with a stiffener, such as a mixture of matt and gloss polyurethane varnish, to set it in position. If sheet metal such as brass or tinfoil is used, draping after the flag is painted can be tricky. A careful approach, bending the flag around a pencil or dowel wrapped in cloth to prevent damaging the paint, should work. An alternative is to paint the flag after it has been draped as required, which is not as difficult as it sounds. The secret is to prepare a paper flag with the design inked on, and then to fold it into shape. The draped metal flag can then be painted from the paper pattern, the inked outlines showing where the design should be on the folded metal.

Flags can be shaded in the same way as figures, described later in this chapter, but this is very much more difficult because of the often complicated designs. A shaded effect can be obtained by darkening the insides of the folds with a very thin wash of black and the appropriate base medium for the paint being used, e.g. water with gouache, but this must be done with great care if the effect is not to be simply dirty and the whole flag spoilt.

Whilst the simple method of painting described is adequate for wargames figures, something more is called for when tackling the larger scales. The usual extra touches are lining and shading, and these are nowadays considered essential if a figure is to be painted to its full potential. In essence, lining is the application of a dark, possibly even black, edge to the edges of clothing and equipment to emphasize the separation between one item and another. This technique was used on the old painted Greenwood and Ball figures, and in isolation looks a little too stark, particularly if black is used. However, if used in conjunction with shading it does look most effective.

Shading is the darkening and lightening of the colours of the uniform or equipment on the figure, to emphasize the folds and creases. A shadow forms in the fold of clothing, and the raised part of the material tends to take on a lighter tone. This happens naturally to some extent on model soldiers, but the look of a miniature is greatly enhanced by the emphasizing of these shadows and highlights by painting them darker and lighter shades of the basic colour. The effect one is trying to achieve using this technique is that of intensifying the appearance of the play of light on the model, because it is a miniature, and is therefore a reduced version of the original soldier. A photograph illustrates this optical effect, and the same methods are used by artists in paintings to make the two-dimensional picture appear three-dimensional. Care must be taken not to overdo the shading because this does tend to spoil the figure, but the line between enough and too much varies from model to model and with the tastes of the painter. It is also important to remember that the shading must be blended into the basic colour to avoid a harsh and unnatural effect.

Perhaps 30 mm figures are the best size to illustrate the basics of shading, but the same methods can of course be used on 25 mm and even smaller sizes with time, care and patience. To line and shade the smaller scale figures, a simplified version of the more sophisticated techniques employed for the larger display pieces can be used. The figures are painted as already described, but when the basic uniform colours have been put on they are shaded with a darker colour. For example, dark blue trousers have the depths of any hollows and creases touched in with navy blue or black, and a scarlet coat is given red shadows in the folds. This darker colour is also applied along the edges and seams of the piece of clothing, and where it is crossed or overlapped by other clothing or equipment. This emphasizes the separateness of the various items. Usually a suitable colour to shade with can be found straight from another tin of paint, but occasionally the right colour may have to be mixed by blending the basic colour with a darker shade, or even black.

Faces need to be painted properly in 30 mm, but again the

PAINTING TARTANS

A. Whole kilt dark blue, overpainted with black horizontal and vertical lines.

B. Dark green through the black.

C. Fine black lines through green and blue squares.

PAINTING FLAGS

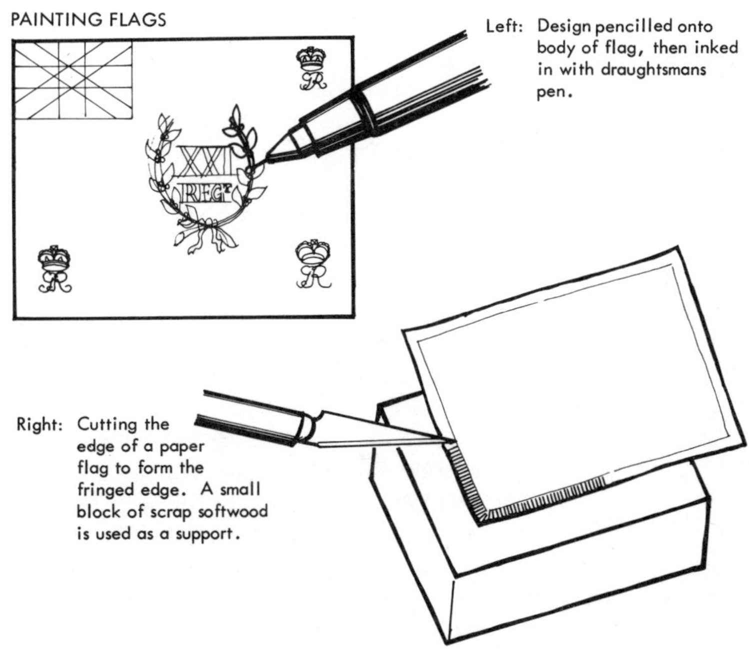

Left: Design pencilled onto body of flag, then inked in with draughtsmans pen.

Right: Cutting the edge of a paper flag to form the fringed edge. A small block of scrap softwood is used as a support.

well-detailed faces on 25 mm figures really deserve careful treatment too. The faces and hands are painted a basic flesh colour, which can be one of the flesh colours as sold or a home mixed variety. Most of the colours sold as flesh are not very natural and, if nothing else, need toning down with white. Opinions as to a good flesh colour mix vary, and the best answer is to experiment until you find a colour which suits you. As a possible basis, try this mix in the equivalent shades of whatever type of paint you are using, with the white as the base colour (i.e. add drops of the other colours to it). In gouache, yellow ochre, raw sienna, burnt sienna, white; in oils substitute flesh tint for yellow ochre; in enamels (Airfix) M7 flesh, M23 golden brown, M1 brick red, M10 white. For darker skins such as American Indians or Pathans, try a thin wash of just the raw and burnt sienna over the white undercoat. The colour collects in the hollows, and the white shows through the thin colour in a very lifelike manner. Negroes are more difficult to paint successfully, but a yellow undercoat with a thin dark brown to almost black wash can work with practice – but remember the palms of the hands are pink. A glaze of semi-gloss varnish can give that characteristic slight sheen which negro skin often has.

The creases are then touched in with a darker shade of the basic flesh colour, made by adding a touch more of the darker brown. The dark shadows are the edges of the face where it meets hair, headgear, or collar, and the natural depressions on the casting. These are usually the upper eye sockets, the sides of the nose, the crease running down on either side of the mouth, under the bottom lip, under the chin, and the ears. Eyes are perhaps the biggest problem of all, but for these scales a simplified approach can again be used. Initially, perhaps, just a couple of simple short strokes with black or dark brown are all you will attempt. With more confidence, suggesting the eye construction in more detail can be attempted. First paint the eye hollows white. This need only follow the rough shape because it is defined in the later stages. Dot in a fairly large pupil with dark blue or brown, and then make the oval shape of the eye with a red brown or dark brown, making sure that the line cuts across the pupil to avoid an appearance of gazing acutely up or down. Use the flesh colour to tidy up the dark line and cover any white outside the oval, but do not hide the dark edging line completely. This will make a reasonable eye in 30 mm or smaller.

We have now reached the final stage in our painting lessons, and are ready to tackle shading as it must be used on 54 mm or larger figures. The main difference with this technique, as compared to the method already described, is that the shading is carried out as the painting progresses, and not left as a separate process after the main painting has been completed. The reason for this is that the darkening and lightening of the basic colour, to emphasize the shadow and highlights, is blended into the basic colour at the edges of the shading to make the appearance more natural. When painting with the ordinary modelling enamels such as Airfix, Testor, Humbrol, etc., the speed at which the paint dries can make this difficult. This also applies to plastic gouache, and Plaka, but once the need to work quickly has been mastered this should present no real problem. The secret is not to attempt to paint too large an area of the figure at one time. This paint-as-you-go approach has been perfected to a fine art by one BMSS member, Bryan Holding of Bristol, and I will explain more about this special technique later.

Oil paints come into their own when shading because they take much longer to dry. Indeed many modellers who use oils recommend painting the dark tones of the creases and shadows, and thc light tones of the highlights, and then using a dry brush to blend the basic colour between from the two extremes. Mixing colours is also much easier with oils because, if a colour is not quite right or does not quite match a previous mix, it can be lightened or darkened on the figure with black or white or the appropriate blending colour. One problem sometimes encountered with oils is a refusal to adhere, and lifting from the surface. This usually occurs when a colour is being worked with the brush, perhaps being lightened or darkened as just described because the mix was a little off. Undercoating a figure which is to be painted in oils with an ordinary modelling enamel (e.g. Humbrol) in a matching shade, can help, e.g. on a figure which was to be painted in oils with a yellow coat, red cuffs and white breeches, these areas would be given an undercoat of enamel in desert sand or leather, scarlet, and white.

Using oils after experience with other types of paints will almost certainly mean a change in technique, but the end results will make this more than worthwhile. Once the basic differences between oils and other types of paints are understood, using oils will in fact be much easier than using enamels, and if your first attempts with oils seem disappointing, do not give up; keep trying and you will soon master the medium and be delighted with the results.

For the benefit of the complete tyro, let us take a look at the whole process of shading. Pick up a bare assembled metal or plastic figure and examine it closely. As an example I have picked up an Old Guard figure of Haslet's Delaware Regiment 1777, in 1/24 scale. The figure is reaching back with his right hand and taking a cartridge from his cartouche box. The right arm is therefore twisted, and the sleeve creased by the bending action. It is these creases and folds in the cloth of the sleeve which must be shaded a darker tone of the coat colour, in this case dark blue. Imagine that we are about to paint this arm; the basic coat colour is applied over the whole arm. On the mixing palette a touch of dark blue is added to a drop of the basic colour, and this is touched into the creases and folds. The underneath of the arm will also be in shadow to some extent, and a little more basic colour is added to the darker mix to paint this area. Now the borders between these three shades of the basic uniform colour are blended into each other to remove any harsh demarcation, but ensuring that the darker colour remains apparent. The same dark tone is also applied to the join between coat and cuff, and where the cross-belts go over the coat. Indeed, this definite edge is best first painted with a thin black wash which will collect in the hollow made by the two edges. The uniform colour can then be run up to this, and blended back, but leaving a very fine black line to show the actual edge. It is much easier to paint the black or very dark edging colour in first in this way, than to attempt to paint in a very fine line on top of the basic colour. A little white is now mixed with a dab of the basic colour and touched lightly in on the highest points of the folds in the cloth, and the same blending process carried out.

The amount of contrast between darkest shadow, basic colour and lightest highlight will depend upon three things. One of these is the colour actually being used, because some colours will take, and be improved by, more shading than others. The second is the figure itself, because if the uniform is very smooth and uncreased then an attempt to add shading will tend to spoil the overall effect by looking unnatural. The third factor is that of the personal preferences of the painter. Some modellers think that a figure should be given a minimum of shading, just a subtle suggestion to assist the natural play of light on the model. Other painters like to use the shading to increase the dramatic effect of the figure by making the contrast as great as possible. Once again, it is a case of trying out various levels of shading until you find one which suits you.

One additional technique which is possible with Plaka and acrylic gouache paints, because of their very fast drying times, is to darken or lighten an area of colour by putting a thin wash (i.e. a small amount of paint with a large amount of water) over the area it is wished to lighten or darken. This can be useful where the shading has turned out to be too contrasting, a mistake which occasionally occurs because the water-based paint dries to a very different shade to that when it is wet.

Not all colours should be darkened with black and lightened with white to achieve the best results. The colours to use, and the shades which will result from mixing different colours, are set out in some detail in most books on picture painting where the whole principal of colour is explained. For those who wish to delve deeper, one such book is recommended reading, but as a starter the following table will give a good guide to the shading of the basic colours.

Colour Shading

Basic colour	Shadows (darken)	Highlights (lighten)
Red	Black, crimson	Yellow
Scarlet	Red, black, orange	Yellow
Crimson	Blue	Red
Blue, dark blue	Black	White
Light blue	Blue	White
Orange	Red, brown	Yellow
Yellow	Red, brown, orange	White
Green	Blue, black	Yellow, white

For black, the basic colour should be not black but dark grey, which can then be shaded darker with black and lighter with white.

Greys are often difficult colours to shade successfully, but if the make-up of the grey can be identified the shading colours will become more obvious. Greys are rarely just black and white mixed; there are usually traces of blue making cold or hard shades, or red/pink making warm shades. Try to analyse the grey being painted, and use the other colours to shade.

White is another colour which often presents problems, but again the answer is that nothing is actually pure white. The basic colour to be painted should have a touch of grey or yellow added to it, so that it can be shaded darker with more black/blue or yellow/ochre, and highlighted with white.

The rather unorthodox technique used by master craftsman Bryan Holding has already been mentioned. Perhaps a more detailed explanation might prove useful, because his methods certainly produce beautifully painted figures. His approach can be summed up as 'paint-as-you-go'. The process of painting is tackled from the inside out, and from top to bottom. So the first thing to be painted is the face, then the hair, then the headgear. Even these three simple stages are further broken down, hence the 'paint-as-you-go' approach.

The face is painted in this manner. First the pupils of the eyes are painted in the appropriate colour. When they are dry they are shaped with white, and the white of the eye is carefully formed. The top edge of each eye socket is lined in with dark brown, the bottom with black, to form the correct pointed oval eye shape. The iris can then be dotted in with black, and if the figure is out in the open a white highlight is added to bring the eye to life. Now for the face itself. In other than oil paints the shading is carried out as the painting progresses, i.e. the nose is painted, then the sides are shaded whilst the basic colour is still wet. The rest of the face is tackled area by area in the same way. In oils the basic colour can be put on the whole face, then shaded. There are three types of shading on the face; the dark lines made from flesh plus a little black, highlights from flesh plus white, and intermediate areas from flesh plus red-brown (Mars red). The lips are created from the basic flesh colour darkened with red-brown and then lightened along the top. Remember the cleft over the top lip which needs the two vertical faces shaded. Hair should be painted a dark shade for the basic colour and then highlighted, and a slight sheen finish looks best.

Next to be painted would be the headgear, and this might be tackled in two or three, or even more, separate stages. Using the Haslet's Delaware figure as an example again, the front plate might be painted in two stages, left and right sides separately.

One half would be painted, shaded and detailed, in other words completely finished, before the other half was started. First of all, a thin black wash would go on to sharpen up the moulded detail of the plate decoration. This would then be painted in using gold with a little black added, and then highlighted with gold. The background of the plate itself would then be touched in with very dark grey, shaded out to darken at the edges where the black wash has collected.

This same piecemeal technique is then carried on down the figure, with a small area at a time being finished completely. On our example figure these areas might be the collar and stock at the neck, the right arm from cross-belts to cuff (front and back separately), the right cuff, left arm and cuff in the same way, coat right and left below the cross-belts, lapels left and right, waistcoat, and so on down and around the whole figure. Even the primer can be applied in easy stages in this way, ready for the next area or two to be painted. In this way the lower half can be used to hold the figure as painting progresses. This may seem a rather laborious approach, but I can assure you that the results which Bryan Holding obtains make the technique worth trying.

One or two more words about fine detailing might be appropriate at this point. The black wash for seams, joins, etc. has already been mentioned. This technique can also be used on buttons. The wash is touched to the rim around the button, on the cloth background, and collects around the button to form a neat black circle which emphasizes the separation between button and background. The background is then painted in the normal way, with the uniform colour feathered up to the black ring. For fine details such as lace patterns the same approach can be used if the engraving is sharp. If the pattern is not engraved clearly enough, then the basic lace colour is painted and then the pattern added with a very fine brush when the base colour is dry. This is one thing which must not be hurried, and again a small area at a time should be tackled and completed. Remember also that metallic lace is not as bright as the metal itself, and so it should be toned down to achieve the right effect.

We have looked at the painting of military miniatures in some depth. Before we move on there is one aspect which perhaps should have been dealt with at the beginning of the chapter, because it concerns the first steps before actually putting paint on the brush. When a figure has been prepared ready for painting, what does one use as a guide? If you have a phenomenal memory you could perhaps paint out of your head, but few of us are blessed with such total recall. I know I have enough difficulty remembering where the information about the uniform in question is, let alone the actual details. So it is essential that the painting guide is readily to hand before the painting begins.

Many modellers find that they can work much more easily from a coloured picture than from a written description, and a number of makers such as Old Guard and Helmet now include a coloured illustration of the uniform to help the painter. If the source is a book, a useful gadget is a holder which will support the book at the right angle to show the illustration and hold the

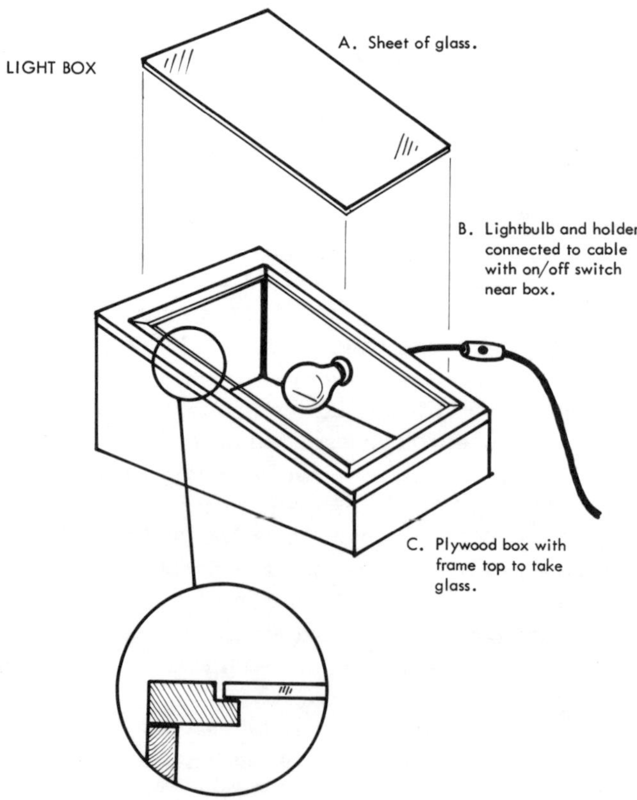

page open. These are available from good stationery stores, the Boots' Ringplan holder being particularly good value. If there is no coloured illustration, only a written description perhaps with a black-and-white drawing, it can be most helpful to paint the colours onto a drawing before painting the figure. The outlines described in Chapter 9 can be used for this purpose, or the black-and-white sketch redrawn onto a sheet of white water-colour paper using a light-box. The light-box is a useful piece of equipment for anyone who needs to draw but lacks the natural talent or training to enable them to construct a figure completely from scratch. It is also useful for making additional copies of sketches. Basically in its simplest form all that is required is a wooden box or frame with an electric light bulb inside under a glass or clear plastic top. When the light is switched on, the original drawing is placed on the glass with a sheet of drawing paper over it. The light makes the drawing show through the top sheet of paper, and the outline can then be inked in. Light-boxes can be bought from large stationers or drawing office suppliers, or quite easily made from plywood (see fig. 4). This is where the water-soluble paints such as Plaka and gouache score again, because they can be used to paint this picture as well as the model itself. The picture can be used to make quite an interesting background to the figure, when the latter is painted and the two displayed together. Whatever the source of the painting information, it is best to check that all the necessary details are known, and one of the lists mentioned in Chapter 9 for recording information can be used for this purpose. It may be that a number of sources will have to be used to gather together all the details, and again a check list will help.

Right, we have painted our figures and cleaned our brushes. Have we forgotten anything else? The usual failing, only noticed in a final check of the work area, is the odd lid left off a tin of paint, or a cap not screwed fully on. This neglect will soon result in a tin or tube full of solid paint, and the unnecessary expense of buying a replacement. To help your paints last as long as possible, always make sure that the lid or cap is firmly in place when you have finished with them. A few drops of turps added to the tin with a pipette (a glass liquid dropper with a small rubber end) will replace any which has evaporated whilst the lid was off and will help keep the air, which causes it to skin, from the paint.

5 Assembling and Animating

Let us first look at model soldiers in metal, the traditional material for these miniatures. Because of the two-part mould used, there is a seam line on the bare casting when it comes out of the mould. Some makers clean off this line, together with any flash (that is, metal which has crept between the two halves of the mould) before sale, and others also prime the castings. Whether the figure you have bought is sold primed or not, it is best to examine the casting closely and remove any trace of the join line or flash with an old blade in a craft knife or a rat-tailed file. All the small-scale figures are one-piece castings, but larger figures can be cast in one piece and then animated, with weapons and equipment being added during animation, or the figure itself may come in two or more parts which are assembled in an animated pose. Both types are available, and some are sold animated or assembled whilst others are left for the modeller to do himself, the latter type being the most common.

Let us take a look at a multi-part casting and run through its assembly. Having cleaned up the figure, the various parts should be fitted together to check the joints. The usual parts which are separate from the main trunk and legs are the arms and head, together with weapons, packs and perhaps plumes and feathers in the headgear. There is normally a spigot on the smaller part which fits into a hole in the body. Sometimes the spigot is too large in order that there is a really tight fit, and the shank needs to be gently reduced to fit with a pin vice. Put the plug into the jaws, tighten and turn. Check for fit and repeat the process if necessary. If the fit is loose this can be overcome when the parts are glued together, or the end of the spigot cut with a knife to splay it. When assembling the parts it is best to try the pieces at various angles to see which looks the most natural or interesting. Getting just the right angle can often put life into an otherwise rather static pose. To hold the pieces together temporarily, use plasticene or blue-tack.

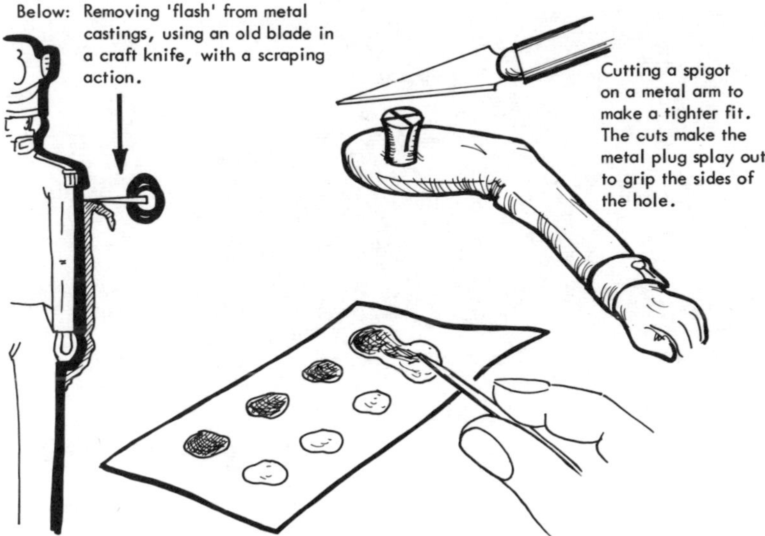
Below: Removing 'flash' from metal castings, using an old blade in a craft knife, with a scraping action.

Cutting a spigot on a metal arm to make a tighter fit. The cuts make the metal plug splay out to grip the sides of the hole.

Mixing epoxy two part glues. The two drops of resin and hardener are mixed in small quantities as required. This avoids large quantities losing their adhesive qualities once they have been mixed.

The best adhesive for assembling metal figures is a quick setting epoxy which will also act as a filler. These adhesives can be affected by a greasy or dirty surface, so it is best to clean off the joint with white spirit or some other solvent such as Evostik adhesive remover. If the spigot will not hold the piece in the required position a clamp of some kind must be used. This can be an elastic band, bulldog clip, a lump of plasticene, or if you have the time and patience your fingers. One of the new instant adhesives can speed up assembly, and the setting time is so short that the pieces can be held in place for the few seconds necessary to obtain a bond. These glues do not have any filling qualities,

Mexican infantryman fighting a US dragoon c 1846 – plastic conversions as described in the text.

however, and there will usually be gaps which will need filling with epoxy putty or one of the other materials mentioned in Chapter 3. When using a five-minute epoxy, the best method is to mix small quantities at a time because the glue begins to set as soon as the resin and hardening agent are mixed. Using a small rectangle of card, squeeze out a number of small blobs from each tube next to each other but not touching. As the adhesive is required, mix two blobs with a wooden cocktail stick and use the stick to apply the glue. Once the epoxy has become tacky it loses its adhesive powers, so leave it and move on to the next pair of blobs, and so on.

Before putting the assembled figure aside to dry thoroughly, it is best to fix it to a temporary base so that it can be easily handled during painting. An empty cotton reel is ideal for this, and the figure can be glued in place with UHU or a similar adhesive, and can be prised off with a knife blade when the painting is complete.

Plastic figures also come assembled or in parts, but not in quite the same way as the metal figures. Those assembled are mainly one-piece castings, either in polythene (soft) plastic such as Airfix or Britains, or polystyrene (hard) plastic such as the Spencer-Smith Connoisseur range. There are exceptions, for example imported hard plastic Elastolin and Starlux figures, which are made up from two or more parts which are sold assembled and painted. The models which come in parts usually consist of a large number of parts; indeed, they are in fact in kit form, in polystyrene plastic. The two main makers of these kits are Historex and Airfix. Almark used to do an extensive series of World War Two Americans and Japanese, and although these are no longer available they do still make some World War Two German Army sets of figures with metal weapons and equipment. A number of sets of other World War Two figures are made to go with the scale tank kits, mainly by Japanese manufacturers. All are in hard polystyrene plastic, but consist of only two or three parts in addition to the trunk, head and legs. Kits are made by Helmet in a soft PVC plastic, which must be stuck with a special adhesive supplied by the makers. The kit comes with detailed step-by-step assembly instructions, and because the number of pieces for the figure is kept to five and the price is reasonable these kits are good for beginners. A couple of failures will represent no great loss and will add valuable parts to the bits box.

Plastic figures must also be cleaned of mould lines before painting and this is done in the same way as for metal figures. With the other types of soft plastic a word of warning. Polythene plastic will not scrape or file. This produces only a rough hairy surface, and so a really sharp blade must be used carefully to trim away the flash line. Hard polystyrene-type plastics are like metal, however, and can be cleaned up in the same way with knife blade or file.

Airfix 54 mm Collectors series are a little more complicated, as they really are in kit form. The figure itself can consist of seven or eight pieces, the whole kit of twenty to thirty. Each kit has full assembly instructions in picture form, and as an added bonus a choice of arms or legs are included so that the basic kit can be assembled in alternative poses. To a modeller already experienced in assembling other plastic kits such as cars, aircraft or tanks, these military miniature kits will present few problems. To the complete beginner they will not be so easy, but if expertise and confidence are gained with the simpler types first, and in particular with the Helmet range, the more complex Airfix models can be tackled. Again their comparative cheapness means that if the first few attempts end in disaster, the financial loss has been small and there are usually pieces which can be salvaged and added to the bits box!

Having gained our proficiency badge, so to speak, the next step is to tackle the Historex ranges of Napoleonic figures in 1/32 scale or World War Two figures in 1/35 scale. It will probably be best to start with foot figures in the larger scale, because there appear to be just as many pieces in the 1/35 scale kits but the small bits are even smaller. An essential requirement before tackling Historex is a copy of their catalogue. This is not only a comprehensive guide to all their kits (and spare parts, which are available individually, a great boon to the converter as we shall see in the next chapter), but also contains full colour pictures of figures made up and painted by the experts, and a number of articles on assembling, painting and converting. This information is particularly useful because the kits themselves contain little in the way of assembly guides, except for sketches of the uniform and some rather quaint advice translated from the French. The instructions and ideas are also helpful when tackling other plastic kits, and the catalogue is therefore a worthwhile purchase even for a beginner.

We have covered the ground in general terms; now it might be useful to run through the assembly of each type of figure step by step, using an actual example. The real key to putting model soldier kits together successfully is to take one's time, and never rush things in an attempt to finish the whole job too quickly. So, bearing in mind the need to take each stage slowly, let us tackle first a mounted Helmet figure kit; No. 16, a French lancer of 1811–15. This is a uniform which does not appear very often amongst French Napoleonic figures, perhaps because these regiments lacked the glamour of the Polish and Dutch lancers of the Guard. The six regiments of *chevau-légers lanciers* were raised by converting six regiments of dragoons in 1811. Their uniform was a combination of elements from other units, the helmet from the *carabiniers*, the short coat, breeches and boots from the *chasseurs-à-cheval*, all with special distinctions. The colour card with the figure shows the uniform of all six regiments, and the figures can be painted as any of these. These regiments are well covered in *Uniforms & Weapons of the First Empire* (vol. 1) by L. F. Funken (Casterman), where illustrations of the officers and trumpeters will provide necessary details for conversions.

Re-cutting the end detail on the Helmet Lancers valise using a pair of adjustable leather punches.

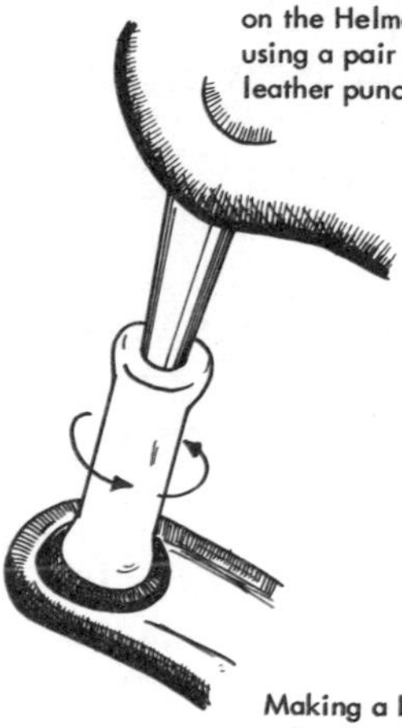

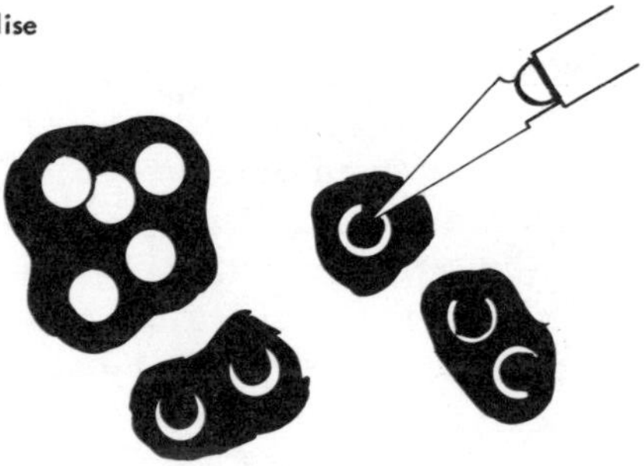

Making a bit for the Helmet Lancer using 5 amp. fuze wire.

A. First shape using round-nosed pliers to form the two rings.

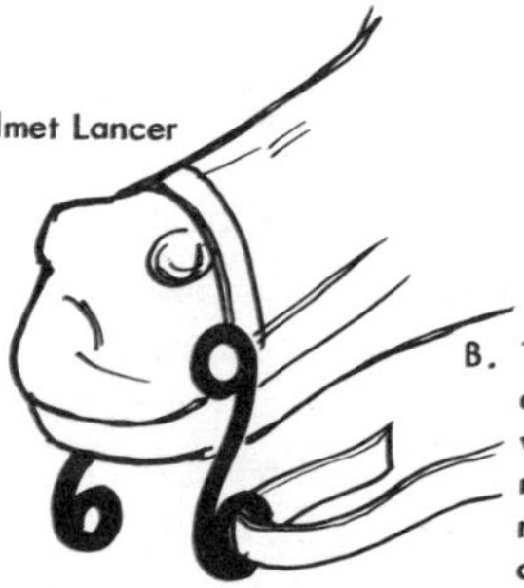

B. The lower rings are also made with the round-nosed pliers. The reins pass through all four rings.

Lance for the Helmet Lancer. First the end of the wire is hammered flat, then filed to form the sharp lance point.

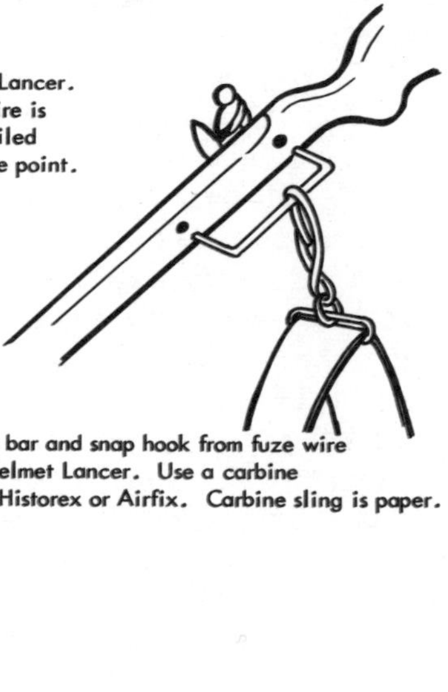

Slide bar and snap hook from fuze wire for Helmet Lancer. Use a carbine from Historex or Airfix. Carbine sling is paper.

The first step is to take the main components of the figure out of their polythene pack and identify them. Check for fit, and see how the best pose is obtained by altering the angle of the arms and twisting the body and the head. As a general rule, a figure will always look more natural if the head is turned to one side or the other, no matter how slightly. Using a sharp craft knife (Helmet recommend the Rexal Versicut with a no. 15 blade) clean all the pieces of any excess plastic. Very fine sandpaper such as Flexi-grit or flourpaper is ideal for smoothing off the seam lines from the mould. Metal helmets on cavalry figures are plated with a metallic finish over the plastic, and this plating must be scraped off any surface which will need to be glued, because the Helmet adhesive will not work on the plated surface.

Cement the trunk to the legs, then the arms to the body, and finally the head to the body. The makers supply a special adhesive, but I have had some difficulty with this and I now use one of the new instant adhesives, sparingly applied. The two pieces need to be held firmly together in exactly the right position for a few seconds to allow the glue to bond. The Helmet adhesive has some filling qualities which the instant glues do not, and so some filling, with any of the fillers already mentioned, may be necessary. Helmet particularly recommend Barbola paste, which can also be used to form fringed epaulettes where these were worn, in this case by the elite companies. If you are not proposing to make the figure as a member of an elite company, the epaulette tops must be removed, and the ends of the shoulder straps trimmed to form the correct pointed shape shown clearly in the illustration in the kit. The waist belt has no buckle, and so a small rectangle of plastic card should be stuck into position centrally at the front. This is the only addition I made to the figure at this stage, other items being easier to put on after painting.

The saddle comes next, and the halves should be fitted over the horse's back to get the right fit before gluing the two halves together. The horse is in one piece, and only needs seam lines cleaned off before it is ready. The plastic used for the horse is not the same type as used for the figure, but it can be sanded with care and a very fine sandpaper, or the trimming can be done with a sharp knife. The *shabraque* or saddle cloth for this particular figure is sheepskin with a notched cloth edging. When the two halves are assembled, check to see that the triangular edging is complete all round and evenly formed. Gluing the *shabraque* onto the horse may prove a little difficult because of the small area actually in contact, and so I fixed it firmly in place with a short length of pin, pushed well home with snipe-nosed pliers. The head of the pin will not be seen under the rider. Now stick the valise in place on the rear of the *shabraque*, where it will overlap slightly onto the horse's back. The valise may need a little attention before fixing, because the end detail may have been spoilt when the flash was removed. The inner circle of the lace trim can be cut back in using a suitable sized cutter in a multi-cutter leather punch. These are useful tools to have in your tool kit, for jobs like this, or for making small discs of paper or plastic card.

The horse and rider are now ready for priming. Handling the rider whilst you are painting can be tricky, and so a handle of some kind is needed. This can be made simply by cutting the head from a pin, pushing the sharp end into the figure between his legs, and embedding the other end in a 2–3 in piece of balsa dowel. The dowel is a convenient handle, and can be pushed into a block of plasticene to hold it whilst the paint dries. Before painting, the figure needs priming in spite of the white plastic. The reason is that some oil-based paints do not dry out properly on the special plastic. The makers suggest U-Spray aerosol white primer or matt white, but this needs to be done before the head is stuck on, as the helmet is plated. I coated both the figure and horse with a PVA emulsion adhesive (see Chapter 3) and this works well, helping to fill any cracks and cover blemishes. I covered the helmet also as I intended to paint it, because to me the plastic looked too bright and somehow out of scale, but this is a matter of personal choice.

The figure can now be painted, using any of the paints and techniques already described. Whilst the paint is drying the lance can be made up from the length of wire supplied with the kit. After checking that the wire is the right length, 2.75 m which is 86 mm in scale, hold it in a pin vice and hammer one end flat. This end is now filed to form the lance head, and the other end is given a sharp point. To give the effect of the blade and ferrule, it is best to carefully file a notch in the end of the flattened portion. A pennon can be made from either the adhesive label supplied or a piece of white paper. The kit illustration will give you an idea of the size. Paint the pennon before sticking the lance into the figure's hand. When the figure is painted, the lance goes into the right hand, and the reins into the left. These are made from paper, coated with PVA, and painted before being glued into the hand. It is best to make them longer than needed, position them, and then cut to length, because the extra length makes them much easier to handle. There is no bit in the kit, but one can be made simply enough with 15 amp fuse wire, using round-nosed pliers. The reins fit through the end rings, and a small piece is turned back and stuck.

Only the plume and the sword are needed now to complete the figure. The plume in the kit is a short piece of black pipe-cleaner. This will make quite a nice hairy plume, but one end needs to be twisted a little to tighten the wire and narrow the fluff to form the lower end of the plume. Be careful to turn with the twist of wire, or it will unravel. Alternatively a plume can be built up using one of the methods described in the next chapter. The sword is a little more tricky. It comes in two parts, a blade with a brass hilt, and a scabbard with a hand grip. Because the sword will be in the scabbard on this figure, the two pieces must be combined. Carefully cut the hilt from the blade, and glue it into position around the hand grip on the scabbard. This is a somewhat delicate operation, but it can be done I assure you. If you intend painting the gold wire in the hand grip, this needs to be done before the hilt is glued on, of course. Next, two small straps to suspend the scabbard from the waist belt. Again, these can come from the label supplied or ordinary white paper. The rings on the scabbard will need widening with the end of a rat-tail file, but be sure to rotate anti-clockwise otherwise the file will cut its way in too quickly and split the ring.

All that now remains is to mount the figure on a base, and label it, as described in Chapter 8. There are a number of extra details which could be added to the figure, and once you have some experience in straightforward assembly and painting, these can be tackled using the various methods described in later chapters. The prime example is the lack of a carbine sling, cartridge box, and carbine, all of which can easily be added if required using pieces from the bits box.

The next step is to try some Airfix Collectors series 54 mm construction kits. This range of infantry and cavalry figures is growing continually. Although it started with Napoleonic figures, other periods are now being covered, thus opening up plenty of scope for conversions. The whole kit is of hard polystyrene, and

French Napoleonic field artillery – metal 'miniature figurines' 30 mm figures and gun, used by the author for Napoleonic skirmish wargames.

ordinary polystyrene cement, preferably both tube and liquid types, can be used for assembly. Again, however, one of the instant glues can be used, and will speed up assembly. One way to help curb one's impatience and avoid rushing things is to work on more than one figure at a time. Thus, whilst one figure is setting, you can be cleaning up or sticking another. Be careful not to mix parts, though, because it could produce a very odd-looking uniform! The procedure is exactly as described before. Take out the pieces, identify them, clean them up, and check the fit. Small parts such as tassels and pompoms are best left on the sprue until required, because they are very easily lost.

Assembly follows in broad terms the sequence given in the instruction leaflet, but it is best to put pieces aside at each stage to allow the adhesive to set before gluing on the next piece. This is a good general rule because it ensures that melted plastic along the joins will have re-set, and can be filed or cut without smearing over the rest of the figure. Using a mounted figure as an example, the procedure would be to glue the two halves of the horse's body together, then assemble the *shabraque*, and then start on the rider before returning to the horse if it is dry. Fill any gaps and again set aside to dry before filing smooth. Straps, belts and reins are made from the thin plastic card provided, or paper with a PVA coating. It is usually easier to fix these items on after the horse has been painted. There are templates in the kit, but assembly will be easier if the strips are cut longer than the templates, because the extra length makes positioning much easier. They can then be cut to the required length, and usually it is best to do this after the card has been glued into position if this is possible.

When gluing parts together, apply small quantities of adhesive to both parts to soften the plastic and obtain a good bond. Hold the pieces together tightly for a few seconds. Do not worry about a little glue or melted plastic squeezing out, this can be removed when it is dry. Controlling the amount of adhesive can be a problem. One solution is to squeeze some glue from the tube into a depression in a small pill-tray and then apply to the model with a wooden cocktail stick or a pin. With small pieces such as badges, use liquid polystyrene cement. Place the small item in position with tweezers or the blade of a knife, then touch liquid cement to the edge with a fine brush. The adhesive will be drawn between the two plastic surfaces and weld them together. This will only work with bare plastic, so if one item is painted use a spot of polystyrene or UHU-type glue, applied with the point of a cocktail stick.

Extra detail can be added to these figures using conversion techniques described later. When working on the figures, have as many illustrations as you can to hand for reference. With mounted figures, borrow a book on horses and saddlery from the library (or better still, buy one for your own library so that it is always available) and study how the harness and saddlery go together. If you understand why each strap is there, and how it is attached to the rest of the equipment, you will find assembling the various reins, girths and straps much easier. You will also often find that the model equipment is not quite right, because it has been simplified by the manufacturer to make putting it together easier to do and explain, in which case you can improve the model by using a more accurate method in place of the simplified one. Understanding what purpose each item serves will also help you to make them look right whatever the pose of the figure.

Simple improvements to the mounted figures include the

addition of horseshoes. These can be carved into the horses' hooves on those where they would show, or better still made from plastic card and stuck on. Make them with the variable-hole leather punch, by cutting out discs the same size as the hoof or slightly larger and then punching out a smaller hole from the middle of the discs. A small V-shaped section must be cut from the resultant ring, and the horseshoe glued in position with liquid cement. The back of the hoof can also be grooved, as they are on a horse, by cutting a wedge from the plastic with a knife, or filing one out with a triangular or knife watchmakers' file. If the shoe protrudes too far around the hoof, sand it back with fine sandpaper. The texture of the fur on *shabraque* or headgear can be improved using a hot pin held in a pin vice or balsa dowel holder and heated in a candle flame, or with the sharp tip of a pyrogravure. Draw the hot point through the plastic with a short, wavy motion to avoid a sleek, combed look. The same technique can be used on hair, both human and animal, but with short straight strokes to avoid the tousled, furry look.

The carbines supplied with the mounted figures do not have slide bars on the side opposite the lock, but are shown instead slung from the carbine sling by a small loop strap around the butt. The slide bar can be added using a length of 15 amp fuse wire, glued into two pre-drilled holes either side of the blank lock plate on the side of the gun. A snaphook is also made from the fuse wire, and put through the plastic fitting which runs on the carbine sling. The snaphook is rather like the type used by boy scouts to hang their pocket knives from their belts, and the open side is put through the slide bar and then squeezed together. The loop arrangement shown with the kit was used, but was intended to hold the carbine when there was no likelihood of it being used, and the strap was attached to the saddle.

Historex figures present the same kind of problems, and provide the same kind of enjoyment, but because they come in so many separate parts the problems and enjoyment are multiplied accordingly! The basic approach is the same; again there must be no rush to finish, and each part must be carefully cleaned. With so many separate parts, it can be helpful to a beginner to assemble and paint in stages. If this method is used, before starting be sure to try out the parts which are to be added after each stage of painting, to be certain that they fit properly and look quite natural. This is particularly true of limbs, say an arm which will obscure the coat front. Check the shoulder joint to ensure that it looks right, because once the coat is painted it will be too late to start adjusting the material at the join without messing up the painted work.

We have already mentioned the advantages of working with illustrations showing the subject from various angles. It is also best to have a definite pose in mind for the figure, and again have an illustration. Sources of inspiration such as prints, plates, and even old photographs should be carefully noted so that you can look them up when you decide to make up that figure or group. If you do attempt animation of the figure you must have some knowledge of anatomy. A book on drawing or painting is usually a good guide, as most contain chapters on simple anatomy, both of men and animals. Borrow such a book from the library, or again purchase your own copy so you have it as a ready reference whenever you need it.

Not only is the physical construction of the man or animal important, but also the hang of clothing and fit of equipment needs to be studied, particularly when alterations to a pose are made. A book on drawing techniques will help here, and so will a closer look at your own clothes in a mirror, or those on your family or friends.

6 Converting

A dictionary definition of 'convert' is 'transform, change; alter into something else, adapt to new use'. With military miniatures, this is exactly what one can do, and this chapter will run through some of the methods of achieving just such transformations. Although a practical example for each material is included, it is the techniques and methods which are important rather than the examples themselves. Using these ideas you will be able to design and carry out your own conversions, and create unique figures for your collection, often at little cost. One question which perhaps needs answering at the start is 'why convert?' The answer is really twofold. Often the figure you require for a wargames unit or for your collection is not available commercially. You must then either abandon the idea of having the figure represented in your army or display, or you must make him yourself, either from scratch or by converting another figure. The other reason is that of wanting more from the hobby than just buying, cleaning up or assembling, and painting, stock commercial figures. Most model soldier enthusiasts are also modellers, so they seek to adapt and alter figures to make them different from everyone else's. And thus we are started on the rocky but rewarding road of conversion.

For convenience, the chapter has been split into sections, each dealing with a different approach or the material of the basic figure, but the various ideas and techniques can be used on all the plastics or metals, scales and sizes in which figures are made. The hobby magazines devote many pages each month to conversions, and although the actual conversion itself may not appeal to you, the guidance given on new methods or equipment, or unusual applications for ordinary materials make them well worth studying. It would be impossible to catalogue all the many conversion techniques in a book this size, and as you become more competent you will develop ideas and approaches of your own. Some materials will work better than others for you, and you will devise short cuts or special techniques to achieve the end result you seek. You will also have your share of failures no doubt, but even these will not be entirely wasted because some part of them will be salvageable and can go into the bits box.

The first step in conversion is the very simple one of adding pieces of equipment to, or just changing weapons on, toy soldiers to make them into model soldiers, without actually altering the identity of the figure. The old Britains Swoppet ranges were excellent for this approach, but unfortunately they have been replaced by the Deetail range which are in the main one-piece models. However this approach can be used on these, and other, toy soldier ranges, to good effect. The equipment and weapons can be from the bits box or items can be purchased from the makers who sell them separately. (These are listed in Appendix 2.) The replacement of a poorly designed and usually underscale weapon such as the rifle or musket can often transform a figure without any other work being necessary, apart from careful painting, of course.

Alternatively the new items can be made from scratch. Knapsacks (back packs) and cartridge boxes can be made from blocks of balsa or plasticene, with flaps and straps from paper or very thin plastic card. Haversacks, which are generally less rigid, are best made from plasticene or a similar modelling-clay-type material. Round wooden dowel or plastic sprue (the lengths of plastic to which pieces of a kit or figures are attached) can be cut into small pieces, with a neck from a short length of pin or smaller plastic rod, to make round water bottles and canteens. For the metal kidney-shaped bottle, the dowel has a sliver cut from its length and a groove filed into this flat surface, and then the corners are rounded with fine sandpaper. The required lengths can then be cut from the rod, and necks added as before. Rolled blankets or greatcoats, usually carried on top of the knapsack, are made from the same materials. Paper or plastic card produce very neat stiff rolls suitable for parade dress, but the more malleable materials like plasticene or Barbola are best for campaign dress where the appearance is often lumpy and far from neat.

The cheapest source of all toy figures to convert are the Airfix 1/32 scale polythene boxed figures. With thirty-odd figures in each pack they represent the best value available, even if only the heads are used! Unfortunately the range is limited, with only Modern and Waterloo period figures, but these can be used as a basis for

BENDING LIMBS

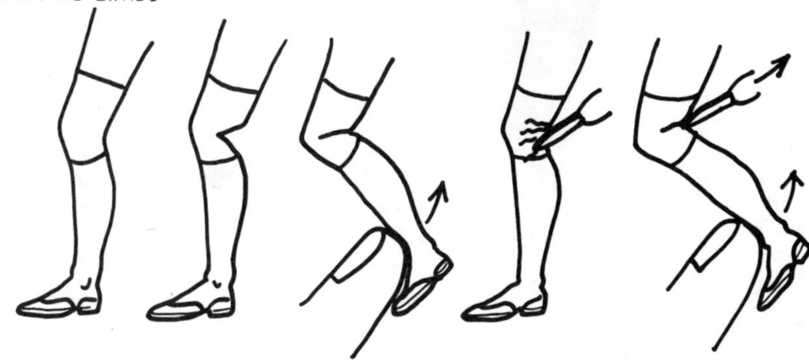

A. Straight leg. B. Cut wedge from behind knee. C. Bend lower leg up to close gap (plastic may need softening in hot water). D. Apply heat behind knee joint to soften plastic. E. Bend lower leg up to squeeze softened plastic, and withdraw heat.

many other periods. Remember that when working with polythene-type plastics, sanding and filing is impossible, so everything must be trimmed with a new sharp blade and, when the conversion is complete, the whole lot coated with PVA emulsion adhesive.

Straps are moulded onto most toy figures, but are usually separate on kits. A much more realistic appearance will be obtained if the moulded straps are carefully removed and replaced with new ones from paper or plastic card. However, the first stage—removal of the old straps—can be difficult and should only be attempted when you have gained confidence. If you are convering a figure drastically, then the original belts and straps will probably be incorrect in any case, and so new ones must be provided.

Polythene Plastic

Now let us tackle a conversion using one Britains Deetail mounted figure and one Airfix Military History series foot figure. The mounted figure is an American Civil War cavalryman with sabre raised on a rearing horse, and the foot figure is a Waterloo British infantryman charging with his left foot off the ground. Together they will become respectively a US dragoon and a Mexican regular infantryman, during the 1846 war between the USA and Mexico.

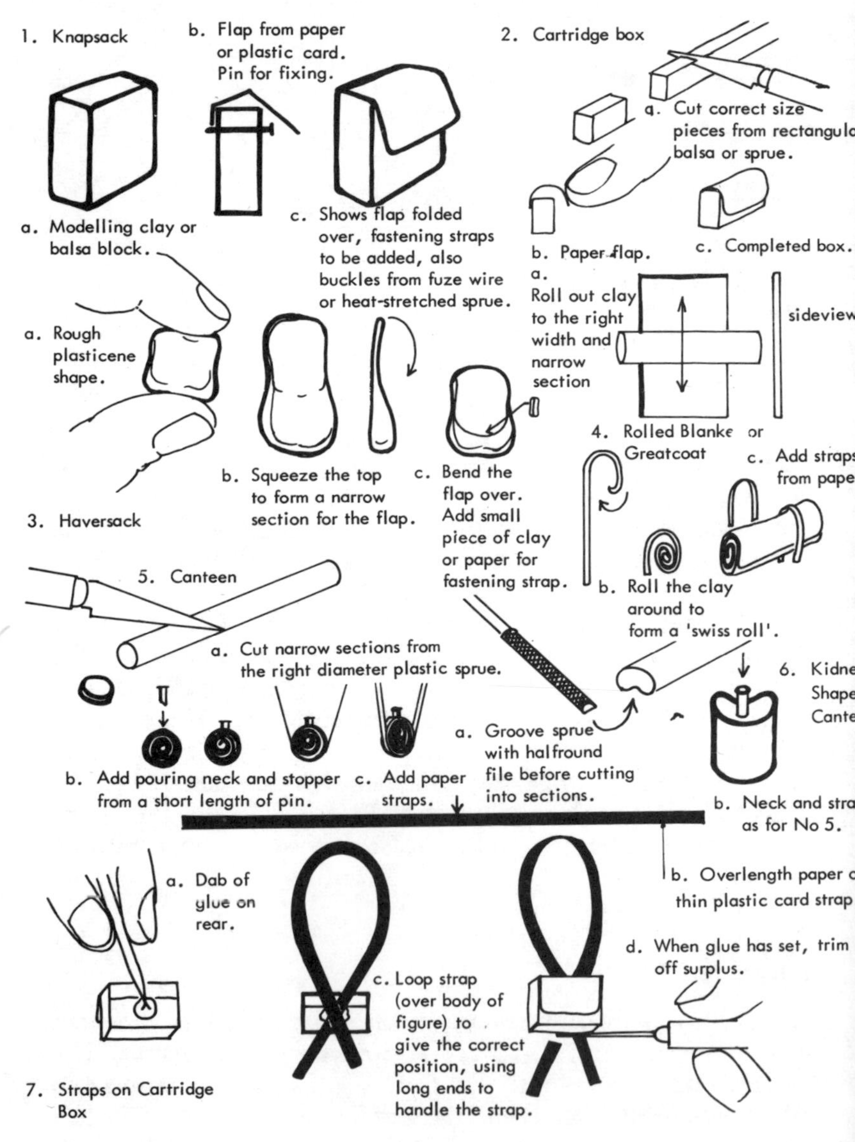
1. Knapsack
b. Flap from paper or plastic card. Pin for fixing.
2. Cartridge box
a. Cut correct size pieces from rectangula balsa or sprue.
a. Modelling clay or balsa block.
c. Shows flap folded over, fastening straps to be added, also buckles from fuze wire or heat-stretched sprue.
b. Paper flap.
c. Completed box.
a. Roll out clay to the right width and narrow section
sideview
a. Rough plasticene shape.
4. Rolled Blanket or Greatcoat
c. Add straps from paper
b. Squeeze the top to form a narrow section for the flap.
c. Bend the flap over. Add small piece of clay or paper for fastening strap.
3. Haversack
5. Canteen
b. Roll the clay around to form a 'swiss roll'.
a. Cut narrow sections from the right diameter plastic sprue.
6. Kidne Shape Cante
a. Groove sprue with halfround file before cutting into sections.
b. Add pouring neck and stopper from a short length of pin.
c. Add paper straps.
b. Neck and stra as for No 5.
b. Overlength paper o thin plastic card strap.
a. Dab of glue on rear.
d. When glue has set, trim off surplus.
c. Loop strap (over body of figure) to give the correct position, using long ends to handle the strap.
7. Straps on Cartridge Box

The uniforms for both can be found in *Military Uniforms* by P. Kannik, published by Blandfords (illustration numbers 289 and 291). Further useful colour references are *Soldiers of the American Army* by F. P. Todd, and *The Mexican Soldier 1837–1847* by J. Hefter.

Let us take a look at the cavalryman first. Having cleaned off the flash, what else needs removing? Very little in fact, just the top 2 mm or so of the kepi, the swell of the trousers above the boots and the rather crude carbine, sabre scabbard, and water-bottle. It will also help when fixing the reins in the left hand if a groove is cut in the fingers, losing about one finger width in the process, and the hollow under the hand enlarged. If a new sword is to be provided, the old hilt and blade should be removed at this stage. Now for the additions. The new sword scabbard will need two narrow straps from the waist belt, one attached over the left hip, one more or less centrally at the back. These should be glued on now, using paper or very thin plastic card, but they should be much longer than will be required to suspend the scabbard, because this will be added after the figure is complete and painted, otherwise it gets in the way and is constantly in danger of being knocked off. For the new sabre, the right hand should be drilled through and a new open guarded sword from the bits box glued in place. A haversack replaces the canteen at this stage, high on the left hip, using the existing canteen strap. The trousers were worn outside the boots and so must be extended down to the feet using plasticene. A short length of pin or wire, bent into an open loop, is pushed into the right-hand side through the carbine sling to take the carbine, which will be added later. A shoulder strap needs to go over the carbine sling on the left shoulder, using paper, plastic card or plasticene. A neckerchief was often worn around the throat, and this can be made from a small sausage of plasticene, pointed at each end. Push the middle on to a dab of glue in the opening of the collar, and bring the two ends out, flattening them with a knife blade or the end of a cocktail stick. The final touch is a new hat, again from modelling clay. The vertical portion of the peaked cap worn by the US Army at this period was quite deep, and needs constructing upon the kepi. A disc of plasticene is then added to form the horizontal top of the cap. Coat the plasticene with nail varnish or polyurethane varnish; and when dry, the whole figure with PVA glue.

Turning to the horse, we follow the same procedure. The

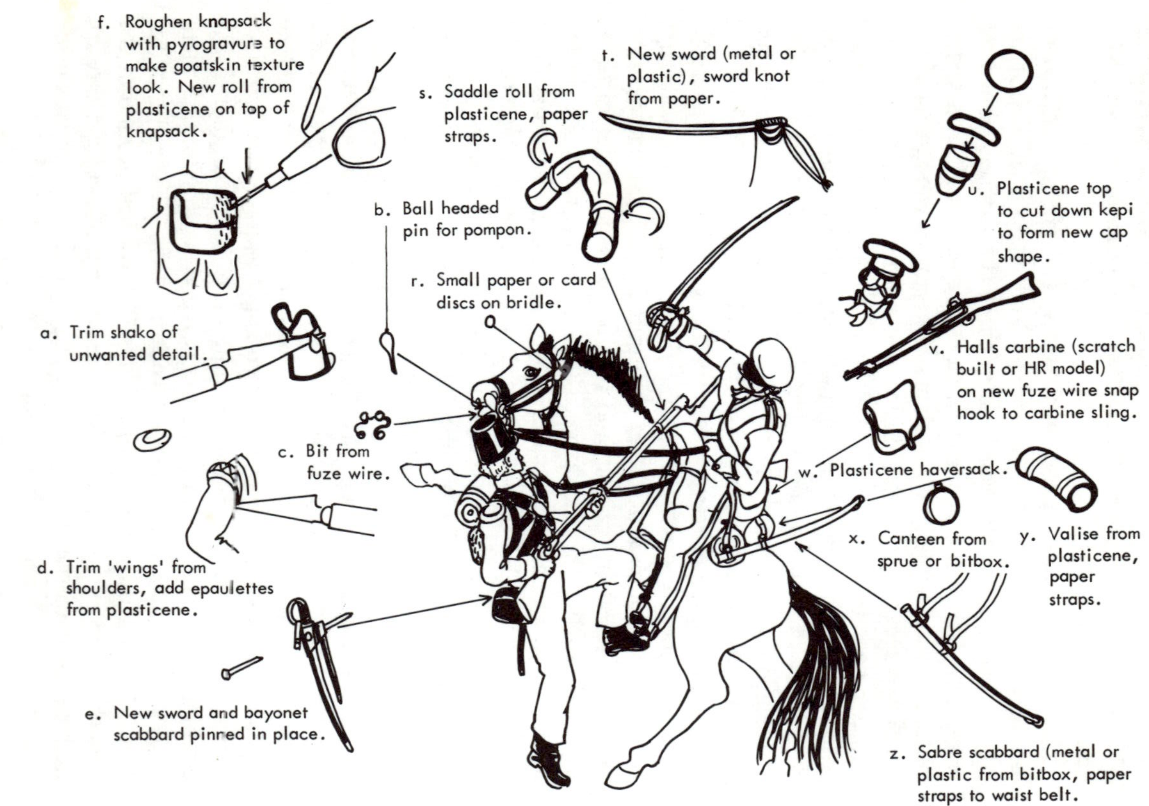
f. Roughen knapsack with pyrogravure to make goatskin texture look. New roll from plasticene on top of knapsack.
s. Saddle roll from plasticene, paper straps.
t. New sword (metal or plastic), sword knot from paper.
u. Plasticene top to cut down kepi to form new cap shape.
b. Ball headed pin for pompon.
r. Small paper or card discs on bridle.
a. Trim shako of unwanted detail.
v. Halls carbine (scratch built or HR model) on new fuze wire snap hook to carbine sling.
c. Bit from fuze wire.
w. Plasticene haversack.
x. Canteen from sprue or bitbox.
y. Valise from plasticene, paper straps.
d. Trim 'wings' from shoulders, add epaulettes from plasticene.
e. New sword and bayonet scabbard pinned in place.
z. Sabre scabbard (metal or plastic from bitbox, paper straps to waist belt.

metal base is removed, along with the plastic reins, saddle and saddle-cloth. The plastic tail can also be removed, and a new one made from very fine wire or cotton thread to replace it. The wire or thread is wound around a piece of card a number of times, and one end is cut through. The other end is twisted together and glued in place in a hole drilled in the horse. New harness straps and reins now need to be added with paper or thin plastic card, using the illustration as a guide. Always cut the straps longer than required so that they can be positioned easily, using the extra length to handle them. When the straps are securely stuck in place, the surplus can be cut off. A bit is made from fuse wire, in the same way as described in Chapter 5 for the Helmet figure. The harness and bridle moulded on the horse are reasonably correct, and can be left. A new saddle-cloth from folded paper goes under the original saddle, both being held securely in place with a pin. Stirrups and stirrup straps are also needed, and can be made from wire, card, and paper, or spares from the bits box. Check the positioning of the rider before gluing the stirrups in place. The blanket-roll over the front of the saddle, and valise over the rear, are both made from plasticene. Finally, a metal canteen was slung from straps on the saddle, behind the left thigh.

The Mexican infantryman is simpler still. Having carefully cleaned off flash and excess plastic, pull the figure sharply back, pivoting it on the right leg to lift the left, so that he appears to be overbalancing backwards. The false front to the shako needs to be trimmed down to match the rear, and the cords, badge and plume removed. The other alteration is to the 'wings' on each shoulder. These need to be carefully cut down to form round, fringeless epaulettes. The look of the figure can be improved by removing the blanket roll and replacing it with a larger version with paper straps, and making the knapsack hairy using the hot pin method or a pyrogravure. A short sword was carried, and this comes from the bits box, or can be cut from one of the Airfix French Imperial Guard grenadiers. Positioning will be easier if the waterbottle is cut away from the left hip and the sword pinned in its place. The ball tuft on the shako is made from a ball-headed pin, with the shaft cut to a short length, or plasticene moulded around the head of an ordinary pin. The larger shako plate is also built up from plasticene. Again, coat the plasticene with nail varnish or polyurethane varnish to seal it, and then paint the whole figure with PVA emulsion glue. The figures can now be undercoated, and

Old Guard Models **(54 mm) Saracen Emir. Sculpted by Andrew Chernak and painted by Keith Wippler. The mane and tail have been modified from the production version of this kit. Photograph by Ian Aston.**

then painted using one of the techniques already described.

When the figures are dry, the dragoon can be stuck into position on the horse, feet in the stirrups and reins in left hand. The carbine, which should already have been painted, can now be clipped to the hook on the strap. The correct carbine is a Hall breech-loader, models of which are made by HR Products. Alternatively the bits box may yield a suitable weapon which can be modified to show the Hall's internal hammer and loading lever on the right-hand side. The slide bar may need opening out slightly on the HR model, but this should be done very carefully because the fine metal wire is easily broken. A sabre scabbard from the bits box, again already painted, is suspended from the two narrow straps from the waist belt. The two loose ends are passed through the rings, folded back, stuck and the surplus snipped off.

The two figures can now be positioned in action on a scenic base, using the methods described in a later chapter. The most suitable terrain is sand, with a cactus and scrub to add interest. The small plastic diorama bases made by Micro-Mold are particularly suitable for this kind of display, and the white plastic can be finished in a number of different ways.

Polystyrene Plastic

The various qualities of this hard plastic have already been explained, and these can be distinct advantages when converting, but its hardness means that bending arms or legs into new positions can be a problem. However, this difficulty can be overcome by cutting a triangular groove in the joint being bent, and then immersing the limb in boiling water for a few seconds. The bend can then be made while the plastic is hot, and when the plastic cools the limb will be set in the new position. When the reverse procedure is required, trying to straighten a limb, a simple cut is all that is required. The arm or leg can then be gently straightened, usually without heat, but be careful not to force the plastic or it may crack right through. The gap can then be filled with plastic putty or modelling clay.

If you have a pyrogravure, then this can be used as the heat-source in place of the hot water. Filling gaps can also be done using this tool by melting a small piece of scrap plastic into the gap, welding it to the sides to ensure a good bond. Do not worry about surplus plastic; this can be cut or filed when cold to conform with the lines of the limb, and used to represent folds.

The Airfix Coldstream Guard 1815 lends himself to conversion most readily, and he is the basis for our step-by-step conversion. Before tackling this new identity for the figure, assemble him at least once as he is, to familiarize yourself with the kit. The figure we are going to make is a private of the Ninety-sixth Regiment of Foot, 1836, and the source for the pose and uniform is again Kannik's *Military Uniforms*, illustration number 282. The uniform is very similar in style, having changed little over the period from 1815 to 1836. The only big difference, in fact, is the shako.

The figure is assembled following the same sequence as given in the instructions, but a number of modifications are made as we go along. The body halves go together without alteration, but the pointed ends to the lace on the coat front must be cut square with the tip of a sharp craft blade, and part 6 is omitted. The legs are modified by having the two internal faces to the buttocks filed, to bring the legs closer together to obtain a more relaxed pose. The resultant gap at the front seam can be filled with body putty, etc. The trousers need to be extended down over the shoes, more or less to the extent of the gaiters, and this is most easily done with the pyrogravure, using the hot tip to melt the plastic at the existing end of the trousers and pull it down onto the shoes. Alternatively, one of the plastic fillers can be used. In both cases the finished look is achieved by careful filing, after the plastic or filler has set firmly.

It is best to move on next to stage 4 in the instruction sheet; the arms. First the cuff lace must be removed; then glue the right arm no. 20 in place at the shoulder and leave it to set, having first cut a groove in the elbow joint to allow it to be bent around to the left across the body. This is the next step, bearing in mind that the musket has to fit into the gap between arm and body. Check this, and if necessary cut a groove with a needle file. The hand can now be closed into a fist, by softening the inside either with cement or with a hot pin or pyrogravure and bending the fingers and thumbs around. The left arm no. 17 follows the same way, with the hand resting on top of the right hand.

The bayonet scabbard and cartridge box go on next, followed by the knapsack and rolled greatcoat. Remember to make the knapsack straps longer than the template to make positioning easier. The best method is to stick the straps to the top fixing first, then pass the straps over the shoulders and cement the bottom

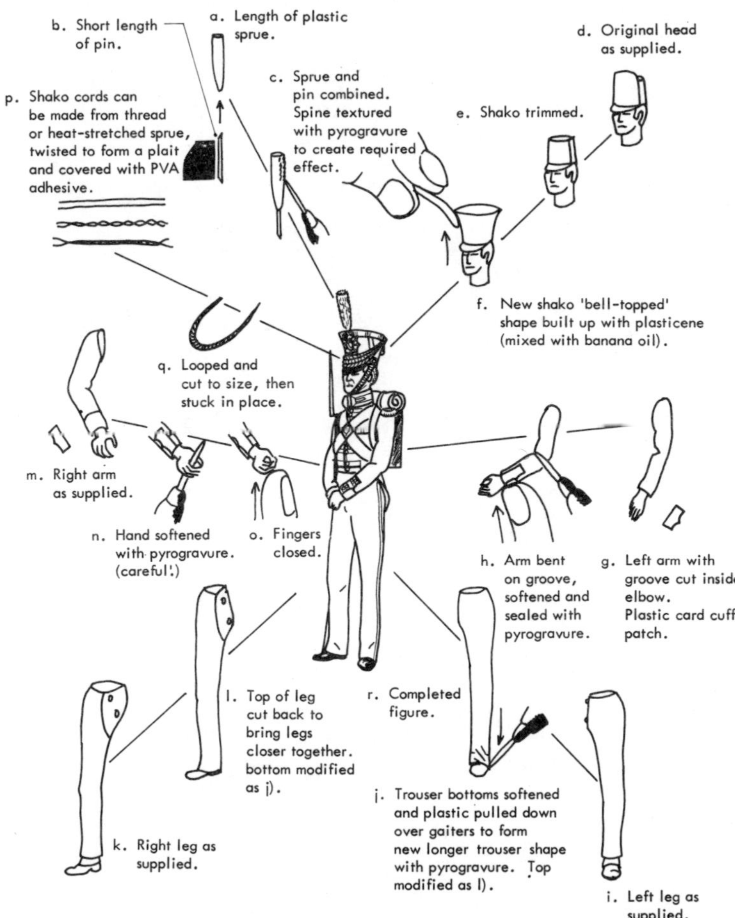

fixings in place, cutting off the surplus strap when the cement has set. A spot of glue on the back just above the crossed belts will help hold the knapsack in place. The rolled greatcoat now goes on top of the knapsack.

Now comes the tricky part, the shako. The easiest solution is to use an alternative head with a bell-topped shako, such as the French or Russian Napoleonic infantryman. Various alterations may be necessary of course, but the illustration shows what the end result should look like. If you do not have a suitable head in your bits box, then you can always build one from scratch. Assemble the Airfix head and shako, but without cords, plume or

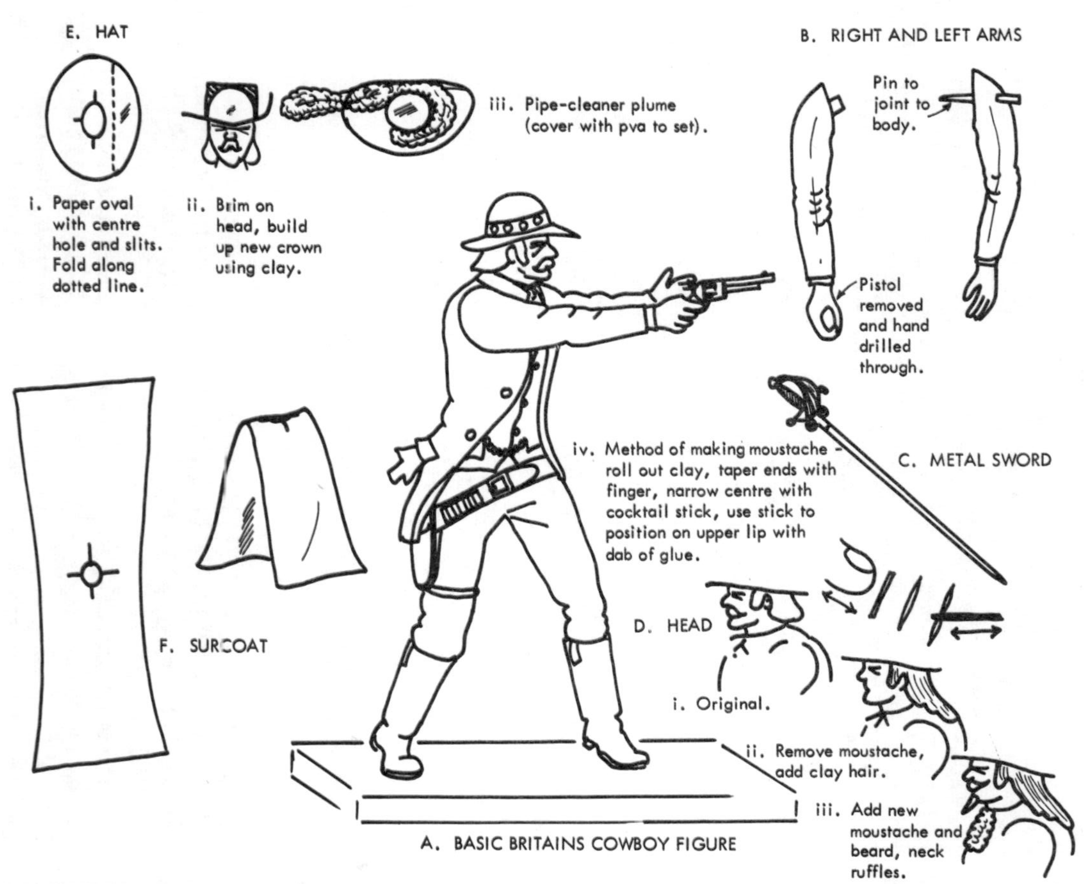
E. HAT
iii. Pipe-cleaner plume (cover with pva to set).
i. Paper oval with centre hole and slits. Fold along dotted line.
ii. Brim on head, build up new crown using clay.
B. RIGHT AND LEFT ARMS
Pin to joint to body.
Pistol removed and hand drilled through.
iv. Method of making moustache – roll out clay, taper ends with finger, narrow centre with cocktail stick, use stick to position on upper lip with dab of glue.
C. METAL SWORD
D. HEAD
i. Original.
ii. Remove moustache, add clay hair.
iii. Add new moustache and beard, neck ruffles.
F. SURCOAT
A. BASIC BRITAINS COWBOY FIGURE

badge. Now build up the shape of the bell top with modelling clay, working slowly and carefully round and round. The rough basic shape can be formed with the fingers, but the smooth finish will need to be worked up with a knife blade or spatula. The top band and V-shaped side trim can be cut into the clay with the knife, or added when the material has set, with paper. The large front plate can be made from clay or plastic card, and the cords from thread. The plume can be made from a piece of polystyrene sprue, drilled and glued to a short length of pin. The plastic can then be worked with a hot pin or a pyrogravure to texture it. Chin scales can be made from paper or card, or as with all the other items the bits box may provide suitable pieces to use. This also applies to the small, round epaulettes and the cross-belt plate. However, if the bits box proves to be empty of the right pieces, they can also be made. For the epaulettes, cut small discs of the right thickness plastic card with an adjustable leather punch. The belt plate and cuff slashes are simply rectangles cut from a thinner sheet of the same material.

Complex Conversions

The two conversions described so far have been comparatively simple, in that no major surgery was carried out on the figures, nor were parts from a number of different kits combined. This is the next step, and although the processes involved may seem much more difficult, they are in fact only a natural progression from the methods already described. Again, cheap toy soldiers are used as the basic figures.

The first requires two cowboy figures from the Britains Deetail range, the figure standing and 'fanning' his revolver with his left hand. The figure is usually sold with his hat painted a rather unlikely red, and we shall need two such figures. Using the same figure for both of the protagonists in our little scene will help to illustrate how conversion can alter a model beyond recognition. The scene we are going to portray is a clash between a King's musketeer and a Cardinal's guard, straight from the classic Dumas story *The Three Musketeers*. In addition to the figures themselves we need two seventeenth century swords (e.g. Phoenix), a pipe-cleaner, white writing paper or thin plastic card, modelling clay, and a new blade in the craft knife.

The King's musketeer is made first. Remove the right arm

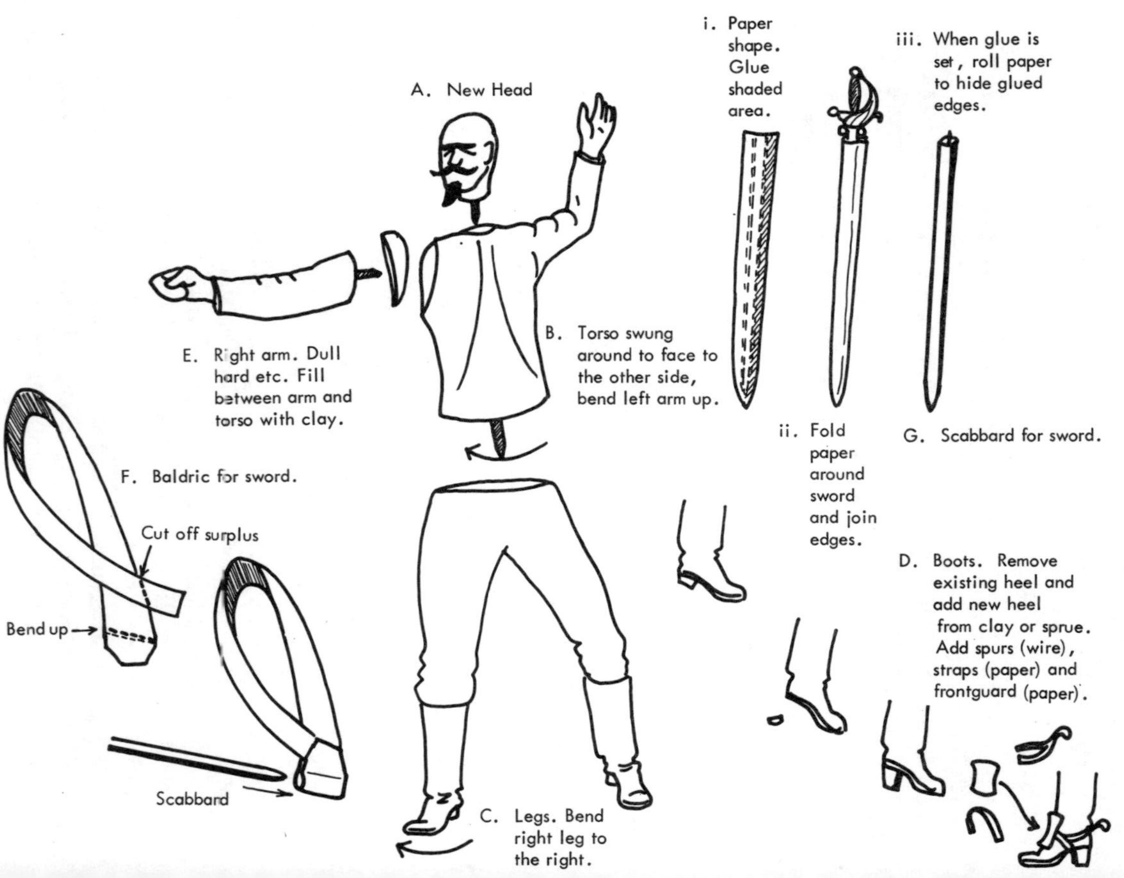
A. New Head
B. Torso swung around to face to the other side, bend left arm up.
C. Legs. Bend right leg to the right.
D. Boots. Remove existing heel and add new heel from clay or sprue. Add spurs (wire), straps (paper) and frontguard (paper).
E. Right arm. Dull hard etc. Fill between arm and torso with clay.
F. Baldric for sword.
Cut off surplus
Bend up
Scabbard
G. Scabbard for sword.
i. Paper shape. Glue shaded area.
ii. Fold paper around sword and join edges.
iii. When glue is set, roll paper to hide glued edges.

A. KINGS MUSKETEER

B. CARDINALS GUARD

THE TWO FINISHED FIGURES

holding the gun carefully; this should be easy because it is only plugged in and glued. The revolver must go, of course, and the hand must be drilled out to hold the sword. The hole can be enlarged using an abrafile or rat-tail file, and the thumb separated from the fingers so that the hand can be opened to grip around the hilt of the sword. All the flash must be trimmed off carefully, of course, and now the major surgery can be carried out. The left arm is cut through at the shoulder so that it can be swung down into a lower position, away from the body. The shoulder joint is made with a short length of pin, and any gap can be filled with modelling clay. The hat is now cut off completely, along with the coat detail below the waist to form the short sleeved waistcoat worn under the surcoat. (See illustration for the shape of the bottom of this waistcoat.)

Now for the additions, starting at the bottom and working up. New baggy breeches are built up with modelling clay around the existing trousers, and tapered to fit into the boots. Seam decorations can be made with a pin in the soft clay. The boots themselves should have the small loops, used to pull them on, removed from each side, and the rear soles cut away so that high heels can be added. New, wide tops to the boots are made from paper or modelling clay, around the bottom of the breeches. Next the old coat front is filled in with clay to form the front of the waistcoat. This need not be carried out too carefully because only the sides of the waistcoat show when the surcoat goes over the top. The baldric for the sword comes next, made from paper as shown in the illustration and worn over the right shoulder. Now for the surcoat itself. This is made from a rectangle of paper or plastic card, folded in two with a hole cut for the head to pass through. Extending the hole with a slit will make positioning easier, and the slit will be covered by the lace throat ruffles at the front and the long hair at the rear. It may be necessary to try out two or three paper surcoats before the correct proportions are obtained. The right arm must go back on at this stage, to ensure that the surcoat will hang around it correctly. Full lace ruffles appear at the throat, and these are made from modelling clay. Now the long flowing hair, pointed beard and spiky moustachios can also be added from the same material. Remember to texture the hair with a pin or needle.

Finally comes the new hat, a much grander affair than the original. The wide, round brim is made from a disc of paper or plastic card with the left side turned up, stuck firmly in place on the flat head-top left when the old hat was removed. The crown is built up from a cylinder of modelling clay, and the long gaudy plume, which goes from the right side around the front, along the left side, and hangs down in a jaunty curve, is made from a length of pipe-cleaner glued in place. The whole figure is now ready for a coat of PVA adhesive (the parts constructed from modelling clay being coated with nail varnish or polyurethane varnish as they are made, if the clay is not self-setting). When the PVA has soaked into the paper surcoat, it can be folded and draped most realistically, and will set stiff in the desired position. When this is dry, the figure can be undercoated and painted.

The other protagonist in this duel, the Cardinal's guard, wears the same form of clothing, and the details of the construction of the costume are exactly the same as for the King's musketeer. However, the pose of the swordsman must be completely different, and this is achieved by major alterations to the original figure. What we are going to do is turn him around to face the other way, so that he can fence with his opponent. When all the trimming stages, with the exception of the alteration to the left arm already described, have been carried out on the second figure, the positioning of the legs must be altered. This is done by dropping the figure into boiling water for a few seconds to soften the plastic. The figure is lifted out using snipe-nosed pliers, and the right leg is twisted around to the right so that it becomes the leading leg rather than the following one. The right arm, having been removed and treated in the same way as for the first conversion, must be replaced on the figure pointing to the right. The right shoulder and the whole of the right-hand side of the body must be carefully reshaped so that the trunk is turned to face to the right instead of to the left. The arm, with the plug removed, is repositioned with a length of pin, and the hole for the plug filled with modelling clay. At the moment the model will be looking rather uncomfortable, because his whole body is swung in one direction and his head is twisted to look the opposite way! This is put right by cutting through the neck, and refixing the head with a short piece of pin to look along his right arm. To help with the change into a different character, a new head from the bits box is a good idea because this ensures that any facial detail is quite different on the two figures.

The rest of the conversion follows that of the King's musketeer, because the Cardinal's guard wore the same clothing. The under-

1

2

3

4

5

6

1 **Confederate Tiger Zouave c 1862 – metal 'Hinton Hunt' figure.**

2 **Camel Corps, Sudan c 1890 – metal 'olive' figure.**

3 **Confederate infantry officer c 1861 – metal 'Hinton Hunt' figure.**

4 **Union regular full dress c 1861 – metal 'Hinton Hunt' figure painted in oil paints, mounted on wooden plinth.**

5 **City imperial volunteers, South Africa c 1900 – metal 'olive' figure.**

6 **Brigadier General in full dress, Mexico 1831 – metal 'HR' figure, comes complete with cactus, mounted on cigarette box top.**

7 **King's Musketeer – converted plastic Britains 'Deetail' cowboy as described in the text.**

7

2nd COMPLEX CONVERSION (1) LYING MACHINE GUNNER

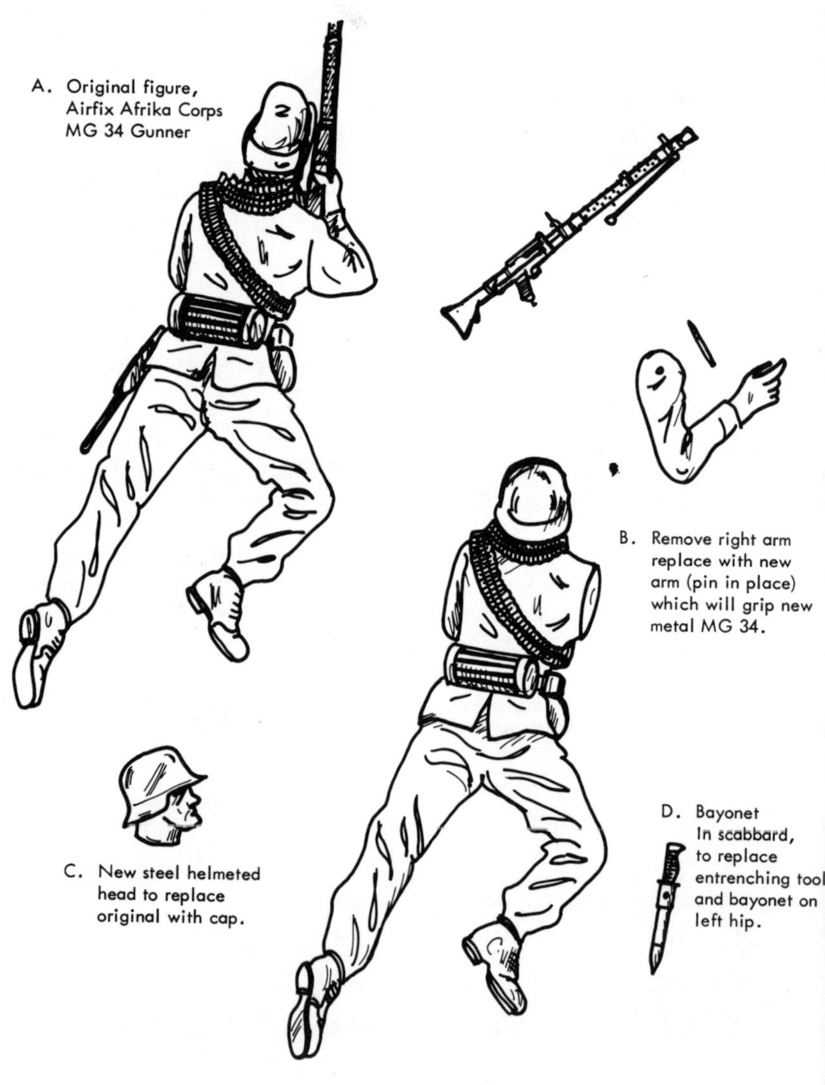

garments, that is the waistcoat, breeches, boots, etc., along with the hat, were ordinary items of civilian clothing, and the only real uniform was the surcoat, in pale blue for the King and red for the Cardinal.

The two figures can now be positioned, with swords clashing, on a suitable scenic base, and the conversion is complete. Perhaps an inside setting such as a brawl in a tavern, using some of the props made by Greenwood and Ball? Or a clash for a lady's favour when both gallants chase the same lady, the swordplay to take place at an appointed rendezvous? Painting information can be found in Kannik, again, and in volume 1 of the general Funken book (see bibliography).

The second complex conversion is rather more modern, in fact, World War Two. The soldiers involved are an Afrika Korps MG 34 crew, and there are a number of books available which show the various uniforms of this famous unit. For the three figures, parts from seven different models are combined. These are two Britains Deetail figures, on WWII German running with ammo box and anti-tank rifle and one other; two Airfix Eighth Army figures, one crawling with bren-gun, one advancing with fixed bayonet; the Airfix Afrika Korps MG 34 gunner lying firing; and a Britains WWII American infantryman clubbing with the butt of his rifle. Let us tackle the simplest job first, the machine gunner. After cleaning the flash off, remove the head and right arm including the machine gun. The steel-helmeted head from the second Britains German is also cut from its body, and secured to the lying figure. Some careful trimming of collars and neck will be necessary to achieve a good fit. The right arm is replaced by that from the American infantryman with the rifle and plug removed, and the hand drilled out so that it can hold the trigger and handgrip of a metal MG 34 (e.g. Lasset). Try out the positioning before fixing the arm permanently. It will be necessary to hollow out the shoulder slightly so that the butt of the MG 34 fits snugly into a groove and appears tight against the shoulder, not just resting against it. The left hand should clasp the underneath of the butt, but as this is hidden on the figure it will not matter that it does not.

Next comes the other MG 34 crew member, the loader, made from the 8th Army bren-gunner. Remove the head, all equipment detail, and the turnup to the shorts. The bren must be cut out of the hands with great care, leaving all the fingers and thumbs. The arms will need reshaping where the gun was removed, and the

2nd COMPLEX CONVERSION (2) LOADER FIGURE

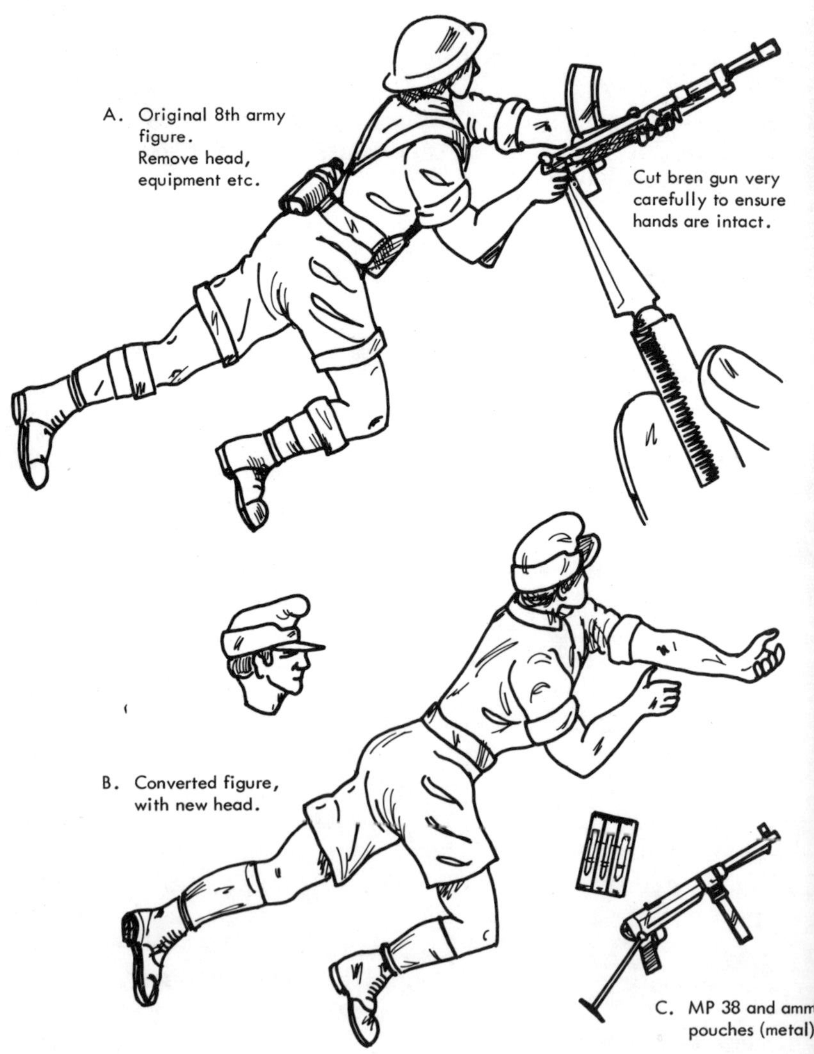

2nd COMPLEX CONVERSION (3) RUNNING FIGURE

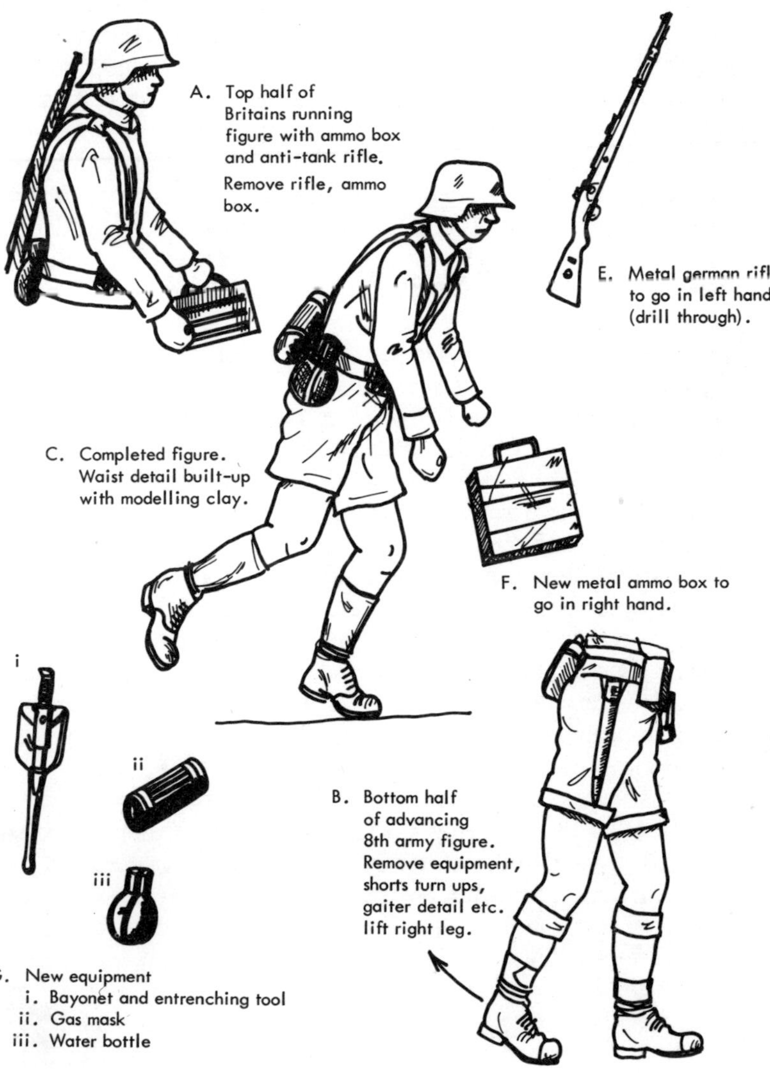

G. New equipment
i. Bayonet and entrenching tool
ii. Gas mask
iii. Water bottle

hands should be hollowed out. A new head now goes on from another Afrika Korps figure wearing the distinctive forage cap.

The third member of the group is rather more complicated. First chop the running German in half at the waist, just below the waistbelt, being careful to leave the two small belt pouches intact at the front. Now trim off the slung rifle, and restore the equipment detail, e.g. straps. The tightly buttoned collar can also be opened out to give an open collar, and the pocket detail must come off, along with the ammo box. Now for the bottom half. Repeat the same slicing in half process with the Eighth Army, but this time make the cut just above the waistbelt. The inclusion of the waistbelts on both figures is done deliberately to avoid the rather short figure which, strangely, always seems to result from using one waistbelt section. All the detail remaining around the top of the shorts must now come off, (i.e. water bottle, bayonet, waist pouches, rifle butt) to leave just the shape of the shorts. The turn-ups on the shorts must also be pared off, and the two halves are now ready to be joined. Before this step, however, the legs are given a little more action because we want a running figure. To achieve this, either use the boiling water method, or the cut and hot weld method to lift the right leg and bend it back at the knee. Securely cement the two halves together, using a length of pin to help strengthen the join, and make good the waist detail and proportions with modelling clay. This latter step is necessary because the proportions of the two figures do not quite match, but the rather baggy look of the German shorts is easily achieved with the modelling clay. Remember to work creases and folds in the cloth, using a knife blade or cocktail stick, and to feather the edges of the clay down over the plastic of the shorts to loose any join line. The gas-mask case, entrenching tool and bayonet can now be positioned. The carrying position varied according to personal preference, and illustrations in one of the books referred to for uniform details will show plenty of ideas. This figure will be running towards the other two in their firing position, bringing up more ammo. The box supplied with the figure can be used, given a new handle from wire. As the box would be rather heavy, put it in the soldier's right hand, and put a metal rifle in his left.

The base for this group needs to be the rear of a low sand dune, with the gun crew in position on the crown, hidden by scrub and rocks, whilst up the slope the hot and sweaty rifleman struggles with the extra ammunition. The loader lies on the left of the

2nd COMPLEX CONVERSION (4) SCENIC BASE

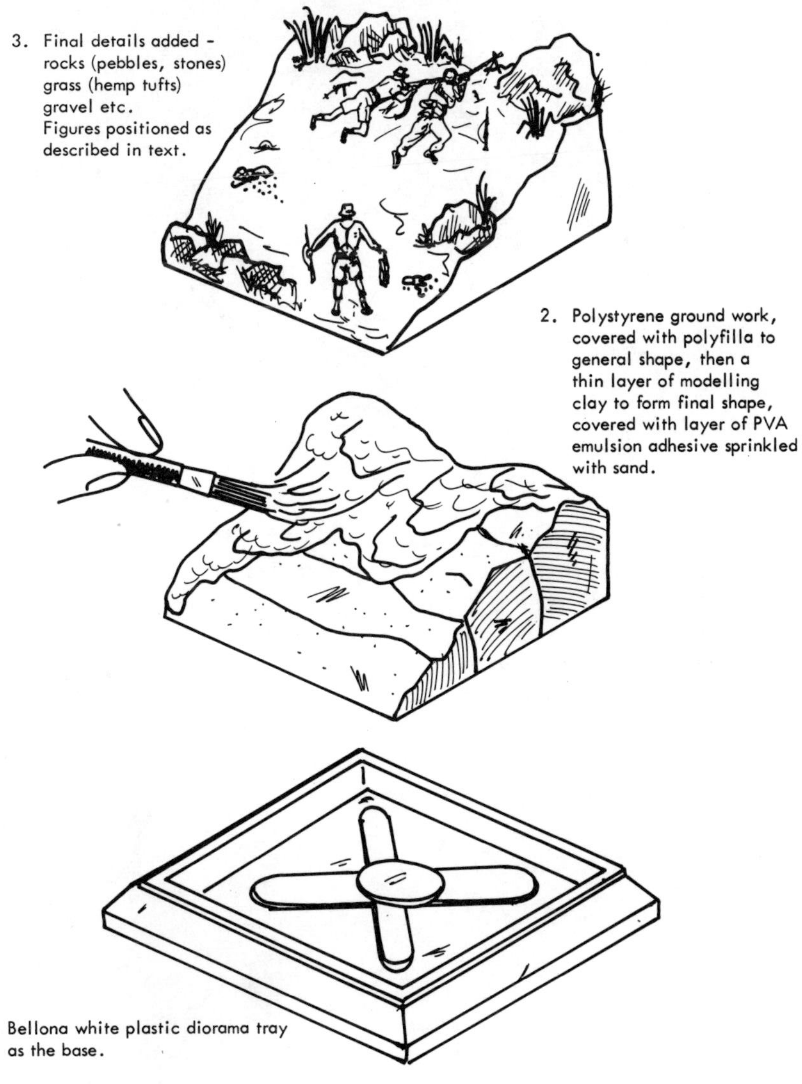

3. Final details added - rocks (pebbles, stones) grass (hemp tufts) gravel etc. Figures positioned as described in text.

2. Polystyrene ground work, covered with polyfilla to general shape, then a thin layer of modelling clay to form final shape, covered with layer of PVA emulsion adhesive sprinkled with sand.

1. Bellona white plastic diorama tray as the base.

WWII Afrika Korps Diorama as described in the text.

gunner, watching the gun, ready to reload with a fresh magazine which he holds in his hands. Scatter some empty cases around the figures and the scene is complete, although the personal arms of the two gun crew could be handy nearby, and other bits of desert warfare jetsam, such as empty fuel cans or a British tin helmet, could also be lying around.

7 Making, Moulding and Casting

Making your own model soldiers is the next logical step from converting commercial figures, and is not as difficult as it might at first appear. It may be that this side of the hobby will not interest you, particularly with so many new figures appearing on the market every month, but you may be faced with the problem of making a number of figures in the same uniform which are still not produced commercially, and the effort involved in converting more than one such figure may daunt you. If you are the kind of modeller who likes to build things from scratch, then the chances are you will want to try making your own model soldiers at some time or another, just for fun. Whatever your reason for doing so, creating your own figures can be very rewarding, particularly when they are admired in your collection and you can say 'Oh, yes, I made those myself.'

If you intend to create the figure completely from scratch, the first thing you need is that book on human anatomy again. Study this, and then sketch out a spread-eagled nude figure, male or female, to the size you require, showing front, back and side views. This drawing is now reproduced in solid form, using your favourite modelling clay. A wire armature following the layout of the limbs and trunk is used as a skeleton on which the clay is built up. This basic nude figure, which is known as a 'blank', need be no work of art because it is only the first step in the process. When the sculpting is complete, the whole figure must be given several coats of polyurethane varnish to form a tough, hard skin.

The blank is now ready for the next stage, that of making a mould so that further blanks can be cast as required. The procedures for mould making and casting are covered in detail later in this chapter, and so we continue here assuming that the figure has now been cast in soft lead or rubber, and is ready for working on. There is a quicker means of reaching this point, and that is to purchase metal male or female blanks from a model

Building up a basic nude male figure using plasticene on a wire armature. The right hand side shows the initial rough plasticene shapes used to create the proportions. This is then sculpted as shown on the left, using a modelling tool or fingers or both, to form the proper muscled body. Mixing banana oil (Aero modellers) with the plasticene before it is applied to the armature will mean that as the oil causes the plasticene to set it can be carved more easily, and is stronger when the setting action is complete

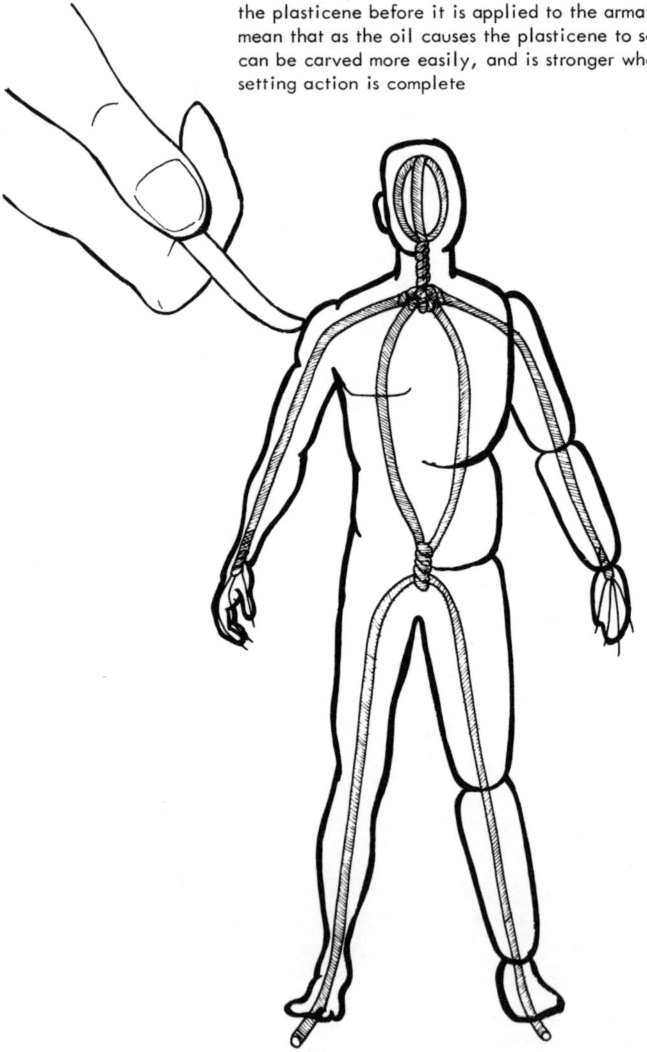

Plaster mould and latex rubber casting, made by Frank Buckeridge. From L to R:
A) A rubber casting, bent to a new pose by means of the wire armature.
B) One half of the plaster mould, with the original master figure in place. Note the extra pouring channel cut between the legs.
C) The other half of the plaster mould.
Photo by D. Wood.

soldier maker. The only company which sells such blanks to my knowledge is Rose Miniatures, and they can supply a male body with a choice of heads, and both a woman and a teenage girl with a choice of four hairstyles. Historex have a nude, but in a riding position, as she is a figure of Lady Godiva.

Treatment of the figure will depend on whether this will be the finished model, or whether a further mould will be made so that a number of models can be cast. If no mould will be made it is best to animate the figure before clothing it. When the desired pose has been achieved, limbs being bent using the methods described in the chapter on conversions, the uniform can be built up on the body. If a mould will be made, leave the model in a spread-eagled position whilst building up the uniform, so that the castings will be in this pose and can then be animated.

The uniform and clothing can be made from a number of different materials. Modelling clays, preferably the type which set hard, can be applied and sculpted to form the main items such as coat, trousers and boots. Alternatively, cold solder or plastic padding can be used, carved to shape when set. Epoxy putty lies somewhere between the clay-type and metal-type materials, in

75mm metal colonial British infantryman by 'JAC', unpainted, primed casting.

that it can be applied like the former to make up the general shape and then carved and filed like the latter to add the finishing touches. The heavier thicknesses should be built up in layer allowing each to dry. This avoids the danger of cracking due to shrinkage.

All the small details can be added using the materials described for conversions, particularly using parts from the bits box. However, if the figure is to be moulded and cast, the limitations of hand casting must be borne in mind, and it may be better to add very small items to the casting. Certainly any detail should be exaggerated on the master figure if it is to be cast in metal, because much of the crispness will inevitably be lost in the process. Detail can be sharpened up on the casting using a graving tool, of course. Rest the figure on a pad of paper or cloth to protect it when working with the engraving tool. When using a steel engraving tool, work slowly and methodically. First lightly score the line required, then gradually deepen it with the tool. If you make a mistake, burnish the wrong line away with the rounded back of the tool. Burnishing in this way can also be used to smooth the surface of the figure if it is a little rough, but do not

Group of smaller scale figures – front row (L to R) 1/300 scale Napoleonic and American Civil War infantry; middle row (L to R) 1/300 artillery piece, 1/300 tank, 15 mm 'Minifig' Napoleonic cavalry, 1/300 vehicle; rear row (L to R) 20 mm 'C-in-C' ACW infantryman, 'Thomas-K & L Company' ACW Zouave, 25 mm 'Garrison' Seven Years War French Grenadier, 30 mm 'Minifig' Napoleonic British infantryman.

overdo this as the character of a figure can be lost if it is too smooth and rounded. When casting in latex rubber this is less of a problem, because the rubber is forced into the smallest groove in the mould by the drying action, but unfortunately the plaster does not always make such a crisp mould as the silicone rubber used for moulds for hot metal casting.

Making moulds, whether of scratch-built figures or of commercial models, is something most modellers want to try, but which many never do because they mistakenly think it a difficult and complicated process. Before we go into the subject in depth, one brief word of warning. Model soldier makers produce figures for the pleasure of the modeller and collector, but they do so for a living. If they are to continue to design and market new figures they must sell them, and the costs involved in the design and marketing are considerable. The modeller who makes moulds and cast commercially available figures must bear in mind that he is to some extent defeating his own best interests, and he must never

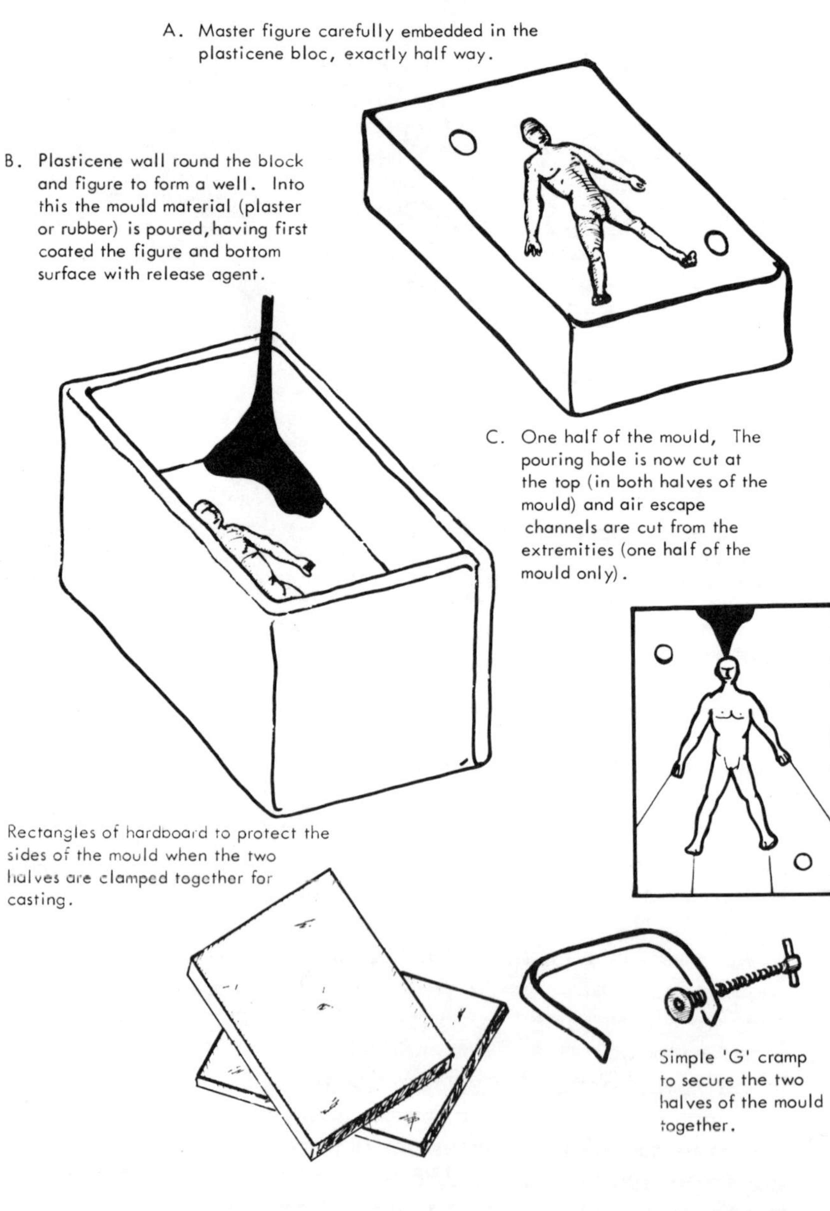
MOULD MAKING
A. Master figure carefully embedded in the plasticene bloc, exactly half way.
B. Plasticene wall round the block and figure to form a well. Into this the mould material (plaster or rubber) is poured, having first coated the figure and bottom surface with release agent.
C. One half of the mould, The pouring hole is now cut at the top (in both halves of the mould) and air escape channels are cut from the extremities (one half of the mould only).
Rectangles of hardboard to protect the sides of the mould when the two halves are clamped together for casting.
Simple 'G' cramp to secure the two halves of the mould together.

produce such castings for sale as this would be a breach of copyright and is depriving the original designer and maker of their livelihood.

The most inexpensive material in which to make a mould is plaster, either ordinary plaster of paris, or the finer dental plaster. Both can be obtained from chemists at little cost, and although dental plaster is a little more expensive it produces a better mould. Apart from the master figure, the other materials you will need are a good supply of plasticene (a hard setting clay is not a substitute in this case), a rectangle of hardboard 2–3 in larger than the model, and bowl in which to mix the plaster.

Prepare the work area by covering it with sheets of newspaper in case of spillage or accident. On the hardboard, fix a rectangular block of plasticene about 1 in larger around than the figure and about 1 in thick. Now very carefully press the master figure into the block, imbedding it to the half-way point all around. To ensure that exactly half the figure is buried in the plasticene, push up or remove the plasticene with a craft knife. Care and patience exercised at this stage will be amply repaid in the finished mould. To assist the keying of the two halves of the mould, push the pointed end of a pencil into the smooth surface of the plasticene to make two indentations. The last stage in preparing the plasticene for the first half of the mould is to build a wall of plasticene all round, about 2 in higher than the block so that the figure is at the bottom of a well, making sure the wall is securely bonded to the block and the hardboard. The figure and plasticene now need to be coated with a greasy substance such as washing-up liquid or melted vaseline to act as a release agent when the plaster is poured on top, to stop it sticking to the figure and plasticene. There are also special spray-can release agents available commercially.

The plaster can now be mixed. Lumps must be avoided, but be careful not to mix in too much air when stirring. A good runny mixture is required, a thick pouring cream, to ensure the plaster runs into all the seams and crevices. Pour the plaster into one corner, slowly to avoid trapping air, letting it run over the surface of the plasticene and figure. Tap the hardboard every now and then, as you pour, to force the air bubbles to the surface and release them. When the plaster is within half an inch or so of the top of the plasticene wall, put the mould aside to dry. It is best to leave the plaster for as long as you can to make sure it has really set—at least half an hour to an hour.

Group of 54 mm figures, left to right – 'Frontier' metal Jordon Desert patrol, 'Airfix' plastic 8th Army (as used in the WWII Afrika Korps Diorama), 'Frontier' metal Chelsea Pensioner, 'Airfix' Napoleonic British infantryman (as used for the Mexican figure in the US dragoon and Mexican infantryman conversion described in the text), and in the foreground another 'Airfix' 8th Army plastic figure (used as the MG Ammo Belt Holder in the Afrika Korps Diorama).

When the plaster has set, carefully remove the plasticene wall, and the block in which the figure is embedded. The master figure should now be lying face down in a block of plaster. The process is now repeated, using the plaster block as the bottom of the well, building the plasticene wall around it, and coating the exposed surfaces with the release agent. Again the plaster is poured in with great care, to avoid trapping air, and put aside to set.

The plasticene can then be removed, the two plaster halves carefully opened, and the master figure just as carefully removed. The mould is now complete, and must be left for a couple of days at least to dry thoroughly before casting. The drying process can be accelerated by putting the mould in a warm oven. When the plaster had dried, a groove needs to be cut from the head, or the base if there is one, in both halves of the mould. This channel should open out towards the surface of the mould, and is used to pour the casting substance into the mould. If the castings will be in metal, it is best to also scratch a few grooves in one surface of the mould only, from the ends of the arms or feet to the outer surface. These act as escape holes or channels for the air which is forced out of the cavities when the hot metal is poured in.

One tip given to BMSS members when making plaster moulds is to put sugar in the mixture, roughly 2 teaspoonfuls of sugar to ½ tea cup of water, added to ¾ breakfast cup of plaster. This is reported as producing a very tough mould for hot metal casting.

If the figures are to be cast in latex rubber, then a plaster mould must be used, because the plaster absorbs the water in the latex solution thus allowing the rubber to set. However, if the castings are to be metal, there is a far superior mould-making substance which will reproduce much greater detail and will last almost indefinitely, whereas plaster will break up after five or six castings. This is cold-cure silicone rubber, which is in liquid form, and which when mixed with a hardener sets into a strong, flexible rubber which will withstand very high temperatures. There are various brands available, and two types are listed in the appendices. The procedure for making the mould is exactly as described for plaster moulds, except that the silicone rubber is made up in accordance with the makers' instructions and used in place of the plaster. The only drawback with silicone rubber is that it is much more expensive than plaster, and therefore mistakes can be costly. A further advantage however, is, that it is possible to buy special adhesive which will enable moulds to be repaired if they split or fracture, thus increasing their lives even further.

Having successfully made our mould, the next step is actually to cast some figures. We have already mentioned the two alternative casting materials. Perhaps the easiest and certainly the least dangerous of these is latex rubber. Supply may be a problem (a list of sources is included in the appendices) because often suppliers will only sell in large quantities. One possible solution to this problem is to share a large consignment with local fellow modellers, unless enormous quantities of figures are required. The latex solution is mixed with a filler to make it go further, and will set when exposed to the air because the water content evaporates. Because the latex loses part of its volume this way, the resultant model will be around 10% smaller than the original figure. In theory a large figure such as 54 mm could be reduced to a 30 mm figure by progressive mouldings and castings, should such a reduction be required. For this reason it is best to ensure that the original master figure is slightly over-scale.

Mix a sufficient quantity of latex and filler, roughly fifty-fifty, although the makers suggest a larger quantity of latex, to fill the mould. To make animation of the casting possible, lay piano-wire armatures through the limbs, head and trunk. The wire will hold the set, but still flexible, rubber in the desired position. Clamp the mould together using elastic bands or G-cramps, protecting the plaster with rectangles of hardboard if you use the latter. Pour in the latex, avoiding the sides of the pouring hole as far as possible because it may become blocked and so prevent the rubber filling the mould. When the mould is full, set it aside for a few minutes to allow the plaster to absorb all the water in the latex solution. The length of time needed will depend on the size of the figure and mould, but five to ten minutes should suffice. Open the mould and remove the figure, which will be soft and flexible. Clean off flash and seam lines with a sharp knife, and bend it into the pose required, then place it in a warm oven to bake the rubber. Again the time will depend on the size of the figure, but when the rubber is a dark biscuit colour it should be set hard but not brittle. The figure can then be put aside to cool before cleaning off any flash which may have been missed, and painting. No undercoat is necessary because the natural colour of the baked rubber makes a good base for all colours. When 'cured' the latex can be carved and filed, and additions made with epoxy putty applied in thin layers.

Bristol modeller Frank Buckeridge has used latex rubber extensively to great effect for his scratch-built models ranging from Medieval to World War One and I am indebted to him for his tips on using this versatile material.

The other widely used substance for casting is, of course, metal, usually with a high lead content. Both because of the lead content and because of the very high temperature at which it is used, casting of this sort should not be attempted by youngsters without adult supervision. However, with sensible and careful handling, casting in metal can be safe, fun and rewarding.

The equipment required consists of a heat source, which can range from a primus stove to the kitchen gas ring; a safe working surface such as a sheet of asbestos, hardboard or a thick pad of newspaper; something to heat the metal in, such as an old saucepan or plumbers' ladle; and a supply of low-melting-point metal. The requirement of a low melting-point is why lead is so frequently used, but there are other alternatives such as Fry's Tanden K casting metal, plumbers' solder, and printers' type, or a mixture of all these with perhaps lead as well. The ideal mixture for your purposes will be found by experiment, or may simply be dictated by what you have available. Generally, the higher the lead content the softer the casting, making it easier to animate but less crisp in detail. Harder mixtures, tending towards pure printers' type perhaps, take fine detail much better but are stiff and liable to fracture when being bent.

The metal should not be allowed to cook for long periods, and should be frequently skimmed of any surface scum, because this will spoil the castings, and impair the flow of the metal into the mould. If large pieces of metal such as lengths of lead pipe have to be melted down, or a mixture of two different metals is being prepared, melt the metal and pour it into the corner of a length of V-section angle-iron. When this has set the ingot can be cut into small pieces and remelted as required. Good ventilation is essential when casting, particularly when melting down old pipes which can give off some pretty noxious fumes.

Before casting in a plaster mould, coat the inner faces with carbon black from a candle flame, and re-apply this coating every two or three figures.

Whether a plaster or rubber mould is used, the casting procedure is the same. Two pieces of hardboard the same size as the sides of the mould are placed one either side, and the mould is clamped together with a G-clamp. Be careful not to overtighten as this may crack the plaster or distort the rubber. The mould is placed on the protected surface, pouring hole uppermost, and the molten lead is poured into the mould in a steady stream. When the pouring hole is filled, return the remaining metal to the container on the heat, and set the mould aside to cool slightly before opening it. Carefully remove the clamp, and open the mould. Inside, snug in one half, should be a gleaming casting complete in every detail. Do not pull it out with your fingers, because it will still be very hot! Remove it by the base with a pair of snipe-nosed pliers and lay it aside on the asbestos to cool. If the casting is not complete, do not despair. Examine it carefully to see where the failure has occurred. Extra air escape holes or channels may be needed to aid the flow of the metal. Drop the incomplete casting back into the pot, and try again. It is a good plan to have a number of moulds in use at the same time to avoid overheating any single one.

For more complex figures, particularly horses, with difficult 'under-cuts', a three-part mould may be necessary. This is made in exactly the same way as a two-part mould, but after the first part has been made in rubber, plasticene is used to mask off the difficult intermediate area, for example the portion between a horse's legs, before the second pouring of rubber is made. When this rubber is set, the plasticene is removed and a third pouring of rubber made. Careful planning is necessary to make sure that the three parts can be held together securely, and that the metal can be poured to reach into all the parts of the mould.

There are now a number of new products on the market which will make moulds in flexible rubber but will not withstand high temperatures for casting. However, they can be used for casting in plastic resin. The main problem with this substance is the length of setting time required for the resin to cure. It does take very fine detail, but the casting is very brittle in narrow sections and must be handled with care. Most craft and hobby shops stock materials of this type, and an inspection of your local shops may prove worthwhile.

A comparatively new venture, certainly in Great Britain, is that of moulds sold ready-made for hot metal casting. A Swedish firm, called Edman, market these rubber moulds, with KG Marketing Ltd as agents in this country. The range of moulds included modern Swedish and eighteenth-century soldiers in approximately 30 mm half round, and cowboys and Indians in something nearer 40 mm and fully round. There are also complete kits which include one or two moulds, casting metal, clamp and ladle. The moulds are very robustly made, and the detail of the figures is on the whole very good. Unfortunately the odd sizes means that they will not fit in easily with other ranges, although the eighteenth-century figures might match up with ordinary Spencer-Smith figures.

8 Displays and Dioramas

All too often when a figure has been assembled, cleaned, primed and painted the process stops right there. So many excellent figures are spoiled because the care and attention which has been lavished on them is not followed through into the way in which they are displayed. It is simply not enough to leave the model soldier on a flat and uninteresting square of metal or plastic when he goes on show. Indeed, an otherwise quite ordinary and unremarkable figure can be greatly improved by mounting on a well-chosen and interesting base.

Display bases, in both wood and plastic, for single foot or mounted figures can now be purchased from a number of model soldier suppliers. Even these simple bases can make a considerable difference to a figure. There are also larger bases available which will allow a small group of figures to be displayed together, and Micro Mold also have a range of diorama trays in plastic which are hollowed out to take ground material.

An even cheaper source of plastic bases are the caps to aerosol sprays, and the lids of some brands of cigarettes which are packed in black plastic drums. Bases can also be made quite easily from small off-cuts of wood, which can often be obtained from carpenters and shopfitters for nominal sums. No preparation is usually required for the plastic bases apart, perhaps, from painting, but wooden ones will benefit from being rubbed down with fine sandpaper and having any end grain filled with Polyfilla or some similar substance. They can then be stained or painted, and the bottoms can be covered with self-adhesive felt to protect any furniture on which they may be stood. Larger bases, for groups or dioramas, can be made from lengths of chipboard, edged with beading or picture framing, or with an adhesive veneer strip (obtainable from do-it-yourself shops) applied to the edges. The plastic bases and caps are rather light, and with a heavy metal figure mounted on them they can be in danger of overbalancing. To overcome this difficulty, fill the base with modelling clay or plaster. Some makers provide a sheet of smooth plastic card to go on the bottom of the base, and this can be firmly stuck in place on the filler to make a neat finish. This can be covered with self-adhesive felt in the same way as the wooden bases.

With a single figure, the base-plate or feet can be stuck to the display base, and the top of the base covered with a layer of modelling clay. The clay should then be covered with PVA glue and painted. The ground can be kept as simple as that, or extra touches can be added to make the display a little more visually interesting. Small pebbles or gravel can be added sparingly whilst the glue is still wet. A desert ground is easy, of course; just sand sprinkled onto the wet glue, and then painted when dry. Painting may sound unnecessary with sand, but it is surprising how much more realistic it does look with one or two shades of sand-coloured paints blended into the surface. Mud is also an easy one, either by churning the clay with a cocktail stick, or by using Polyfilla in place of the plasticene, and modelling to look like disturbed earth. Grass is rather more difficult. Model railway materials can come in useful here, in particular the various coloured sawdusts and flocks which can be sprinkled on to the wet glue to texture it as short grass. Tufts of longer grass can be represented with short lengths of hemp rope, bristles from old paint brushes, or even bits of real grass, all cemented into holes made in the clay with a pointed trowel.

Small bushes are best made from lichen, the strange rubbery stuff sold for model railways and wargamers. An internal branch structure may be necessary, depending on the size and type of bush being represented. This can be made from dried twigs from small garden plants or weeds. Larger trees are best left for dioramas, but a single tree stump or blasted trunk can look quite effective, and can again be made from a piece of dried twig. Bryan Holding of Bristol often embellishes his bases, particularly those of large scale 75/77 mm figures, to great effect with small cacti from his collection.

A man-made surface such as cobblestones, paving or tarmac may be required. All these and many others can be represented with a little imagination and care. For cobblestones, use dried lentils or split peas placed flat side down on a layer of PVA glue, but be careful how the figure or figures are stood on the stones. Remember that their boots should be on top of the cobbles, not in amongst them. Flagstones and paving stones can easily be made by

Old Guard Models **(54 mm) MG 34 team and NCO. Designed by William Murray and painted by Malcolm Dawson. The photograph shows how effective scenery can be made from common household items. The long grass is made from sisal string pressed into wet plaster. Photo by Ian Aston.**

using card or plastic card cut into the appropriate size pieces and then glued in place, or one of the embossed plastic card sheets can be used. Tarmac is, oddly enough, one of the more difficult surfaces to reproduce in miniature, because the texture is very slight but is very familiar to everyone. Fine sand with a thin wash of PVA emulsion glue can look quite effective, but tarmac can be suggested almost as well simply by painting, remembering that it is various shades of grey, not black. With the other surfaces, a thin wash of the darkest colouring present in the surface, or even very dark grey or brown, spread over the whole area, will run down into the hollows and emphasize the texture. The main colours can then be applied with an almost dry brush over the raised parts of the area.

A great number of the small bits and pieces which can be put on the base to add interest or to help set the scene can be found in the garden or roadside. Small stones, pebbles, gravel, twigs and grass are all readily available to anyone, even in towns. Apart from model shops, especially those dealing with model railways, there are two other specialist shops which are worth investigating when seeking items to enhance display bases. These are florists selling flower arranging materials, and pet or tropical fish shops who have aquarium decorations. Flower arranging materials particularly suitable for our purposes are the many different dried flower heads, seed pods and grasses, bark and even plastic flowers. From the aquarium there are many different gravels, in natural and dyed colours, small pieces of stone, man-made items such as plaster walls and ruins, and the exotic plastic underwater plants which can look very effective, repainted as tropical jungle blooms and undergrowth.

All sorts of unlikely items can be used, and, as with the various bits and pieces from the models themselves, never throw anything away. Storing all these small items such as sand, gravel and dried flowers can be a problem. One solution is to use empty glass screw-top jars. These are usually readily available in the home, and the contents can be seen through the glass, thus aiding the selection of the right material.

Apart from natural additions such as those already described, there are other man-made objects which can be added to the display base. These are small pieces of equipment or clothing, the battlefield debris which so often littered the ground both during and after a battle. A broken gun wheel, an abandoned shako or pack, even a rifle or sword dropped by a wounded soldier or discarded in flight by the defeated army—little touches which can add an extra something to the display.

Apart from simply putting these bits and pieces on the base with the figure, they can be made a more integral part of the display. A figure can be given a raised leg, bent at the knee, and the foot can be placed on a rock, log or even wheel, say; of an officer might be examining an enemy helmet or shako. Seat or lean a weary soldier against a wall in the shade, or animate a horse to catch it in the act of leaping a hedge or gate. There is no real limit to what can be done quite simply, and which will add that little extra life to the display.

The next step from single figure or small groups just displayed on a common base is to make the models and their base into a picture, to actually portray a scene in the same way as a painting or photograph. Instead of paint and brush, or camera and film, three-dimensional model soldiers are used to capture a moment in time from a battle, a parade or just an incident in the life of an army. This is an aspect of the hobby to which more and more modellers are turning, in an attempt to extend their interests and make their display or collection really tell a story. These scenes are usually called dioramas, and they employ all the ideas mentioned for scenic bases, plus some additional problems and solutions.

It is even more important to have a clear idea of what you hope to achieve with a diorama than it is with individual figures or groups. Careful thought and preparatory planning will be repaid during the construction stages, because possible pitfalls will have been foreseen, and a solution found, before work is even started. The figures are put together, and can be painted in exactly the same way as for individual display pieces. However, because there are often large numbers of figures involved, many modellers do not attempt to achieve as high a standard of painting with each figure as they would with single display pieces, because they aim for an overall effect rather than individual perfection.

Let us take a look at the stages in planning and constructing a diorama, using as an example of the methods a small set-piece of mine. This was a small diorama, only 320 mm by 220 mm. It was initially constructed for display at a BMSS Bristol branch annual show, and subsequently I was fortunate enough to win a prize with it in the annual BMSS competitions. The figures are all 30 mm 'Willie' figures, from the Dolly Grey range.

The first step was to decide on the period for the diorama. This was easy because the Sudan is one of my favourite Colonial periods, and so an incident from the River War was chosen, with dervishes, fuzzy-wuzzies and the 21st Lancers. The Suren catalogue was consulted, and a selection made of figures from which the protagonists could be chosen. There being no definite incident in my mind I was free to leave the choice of figures to my fancy in this way. Had I decided upon a more positive incident which was represented in a painting or photograph, then the figures would have been chosen using the original portrayal as a guide, and the requisite number of types, and suitable poses or figures which would lend themselves to re-animation in the correct poses, would have been selected.

This is very often the way in which modellers settle on a particular incident; inspired by the picture or photograph. This is in fact very good discipline, because there are usually a number of figures which have to be animated or converted to achieve the right poses, and working in this way to obtain a well-defined pose is both taxing and stimulating. It also makes the planning of the layout of the diorama much easier because the ground plan is already designed, and if the two-dimensional picture is visually interesting then it follows that the three-dimensional picture based on it will be also. If the original inspiration contains a very large number of figures, it may be necessary to select the main features and do no more than suggest the other areas. One way in which larger masses of soldiers in the background and an idea of distance and depth can be suggested quite effectively is by the use of figures to more than one scale. The foreground figures can be 54 mm, other figures in the middle of the scene can be 30 mm, and soldiers in the distance can be 20 mm. This reduction in size gives the appearance of perspective when the ground and scenery are scaled in the same way. This is not an easy effect to achieve, however, and is certainly not for beginners.

Having selected our figures, based either on the picture which inspired the diorama or our own personal ideas, the next step is to work out the terrain on which they are to be displayed, and the methods of constructing it. Size is usually the main restriction. Most of us would like to build a diorama 8 ft by 8 ft but having nowhere to put such a monster we end up with one nearer 8 in by 8 in. Should you be lucky enough to have a suitable location for a large diorama, then there is no physical difficulty in constructing one to virtually any size. Weight is the next consideration. There are two possible solutions to the weight problem. One is to use traditional construction methods employed by model railway enthusiasts for their layouts which often have to be moved around the country. These methods involve the construction of an under-framework of battens on which chicken-wire is nailed, moulded to the correct shape and covered with *papier mâché*. These methods are described in detail in many books on model railways, and two readily available ones arc listed in the appendices.

The other solution is a more modern one, using one of the new materials now easily obtained at little cost: expanded polystyrene. Using sheets, tiles or blocks of this very light but quite robust substance, the main shape of the terrain for the diorama can be carved out. The polystyrene can be cut quite easily with a really sharp knife. If the size is such that it will tend to flex or warp along its length without support, a panel of hardboard used as a base should suffice. The polystyrene can be stuck to the hardboard, and to itself, with a special cement, or a cheaper method is to use a thin mix of Polyfilla. When the basic shape has been obtained, the whole surface of the polystyrene is covered with a layer of Polyfilla. This can be textured or smoothed to make the various natural surfaces required. The Polyfilla should be quite thin, and is applied with a paintbrush. The size of the brush will depend on the size of the diorama, but a 1-in brush will tackle most areas. The figures can be positioned in the wet Polyfilla, and their bases hidden by bringing the plaster carefully around their feet with an artists' brush. One coating of Polyfilla may be enough, but if a second coat will be required it must be applied very carefully around the figures.

Natural items such as rocks, bushes and trees, and long grass, and man-made items such as fences and buildings, all of which sit on the surface of the terrain, can also be positioned in the wet plaster. This will make them look like an integral part of the scene, with the earth tending to lap up around them as it does in real life.

It is best to work out the general shape of the terrain and the positions of figures and accessories on paper, preferably the same size as the diorama. This will help to identify any problem areas, overcrowding of figures for example, and allow you to adjust both ground and figures before any permanent work starts. When the layout is planned, build up the rough shape of the ground and carve to achieve the required terrain. Make a final check with the figures in their proposed positions before applying the Polyfilla.

There is another method of constructing the terrain for a diorama. Where weight is less of a problem, for example with smaller sizes, the ground can be built up with modelling clay. The clay can either be used on its own, or a sub-structure of wooden blocks can be used to form the rough basic shape. These blocks can be glued or pinned in position, and clay moulded over them to form the shape of the ground. This is the method I used for my Sudan diorama because of its size. Let us take a look at this practical example, having completed the stages described so far.

Having decided upon the theme, the next step was to select suitable figures. I pictured an incident during a scouting patrol, with five lancers suddenly confronted with a group of the Mahdi's army. The five lancers consisted of an officer, NCO, and three troopers. The officer and NCO carried swords, and the troopers had lances. Two of the troopers were in the attack position and one was recovering his lance. For the Mahdists, there was one

Jehediya rifleman, one standard bearer, two dervishes in jibbas armed with spears, eight fuzzy-wuzzies in various poses and armed with their razor-sharp swords, and an emir on foot with spears and a sword. I gave some of the fuzzy-wuzzies additional knives made from copper staples filed to shape. These were tucked into their waistbands by using plastic padding both to stick the knife in position and to take the waistband around it.

Playing around with the figures, trying them together in various combinations, soon produced some good groupings. For example, one Sudanese was crouched low, and an attacking trooper's lance just skimmed over his head, so that the fuzzy-wuzzy appeared to have just dodged beneath the lance and was now ready to swing his huge sword up at the unprotected lancer! The terrain plan has a dip to the near right-hand corner to suggest a wadi, with a few rocks to the far left in which the rifleman could lurk, waiting to shoot the lancers in the back as they charged down into the wadi. Around the rocks there would be a few brown clumps of scrub, parched and dry in the hot sun. The tray in which the diorama was constructed was made from a rectangle of hardboard with a $\frac{3}{4}$ in by $\frac{1}{4}$ in batten mitred frame pinned to it. The frame was finished by sanding and sealing with polyurethane varnish.

To build up the approximate shape of the ground, an assortment of odd pieces of wood were bluetacked in place, and the whole area was covered with a layer of plasticene. The figures were firmly embedded into this, making sure their bases were hidden. The plasticene was then covered with a coat of PVA emulsion glue, and sand was sprinkled over it whilst it was wet. Small rocks were added using aquarium gravel, extra PVA being used where necessary. The larger rocks were just stones from the garden, with brown lichen for scrub, and again both were stuck in place with PVA. When the PVA was dry the sand was coloured with enamel paints well thinned with turps. A darker mix, made by adding a little black, was used in the hollows to emphasize them, and lighter washes applied over the rest of the surface.

The methods of finishing the surface to represent sand, grass, earth, etc., have already been described for individual bases, and the same methods are used for the larger areas of a diorama. Painting these surfaces to look realistic can be a problem. One thing to remember is that, when you are looking at a diorama, it is as if you were viewing the scene in real life from a distance, and this means that the ground colours are more subtle than when seen

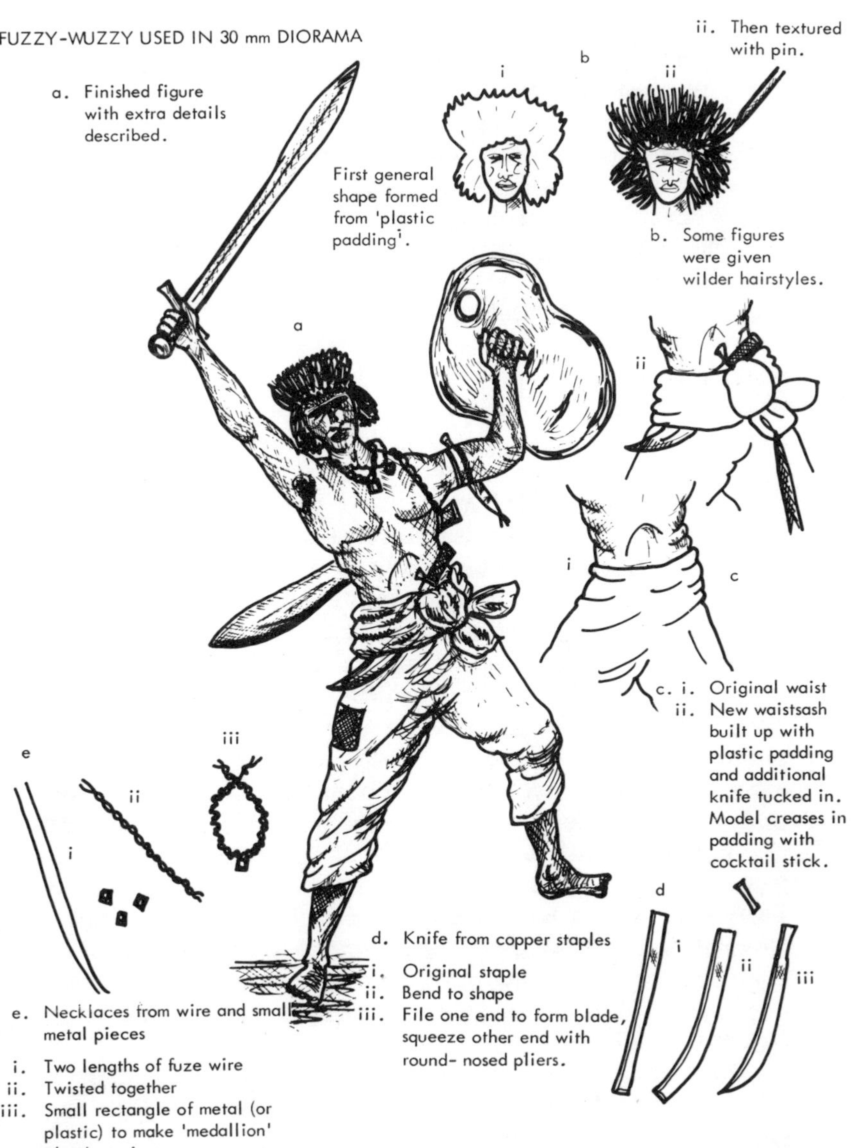
FUZZY-WUZZY USED IN 30 mm DIORAMA
a. Finished figure with extra details described.
b
i
ii
ii. Then textured with pin.
First general shape formed from 'plastic padding'.
b. Some figures were given wilder hairstyles.
a
ii
i
c
c. i. Original waist
ii. New waistsash built up with plastic padding and additional knife tucked in. Model creases in padding with cocktail stick.
e
iii
ii
i
d
i
ii
iii
d. Knife from copper staples
i. Original staple
ii. Bend to shape
iii. File one end to form blade, squeeze other end with round- nosed pliers.
e. Necklaces from wire and small metal pieces
i. Two lengths of fuze wire
ii. Twisted together
iii. Small rectangle of metal (or plastic) to make 'medallion' glued to wire.

close up. Grassed surfaces can be coloured using only two or three colours, and everyday household emulsion paint is the best value. The basic ground colour is a khaki, brown or olive. This is then worked over with a dark green, blending the two colours liberally leaving the base colour to show through in patches. A lighter green can then go on top of these two colours, again in patches on the higher ground, but well blended to lose any hard edges. The surface texturing, such as coloured sawdust or flock, can go on before or after painting. If it goes on afterwards it may need toning down a little, because some of the colours used in dying it are rather bright. The wet emulsion is usually sufficient to hold the sawdust sprinkled on to it.

Special effects, particularly water, can be tricky. Muddy water such as gathers in the bottom of puddles, shell holes or trenches is reasonably easy. The water depth is made with plaster or clay. The area underwater is painted a murky brown, and then gloss varnished to obtain the light-reflecting surface of the water. Clear water, particularly running water, is rather more difficult. Perhaps the most realistic-looking model water is made by using a clear plastic resin of the kind used for plastic casting, such as that marketed by Isopon. The bed of the river or stream is constructed in the same way as the ground, with a smooth, rough, or rock-strewn surface as appropriate to the kind of stretch of water being represented. The banks need particularly careful treatment, bearing in mind that there is usually a definite edge and often an overhang, and so they are best finished after the water has been completed. Make sure that the ends of the run of water are sealed, and just pour in the clear resin to the required level. A slight grey/blue tint to the clear plastic will help to soften the effect of a considerable depth of plastic. The resin can also be tinted progressively, lightening it as it nears the surface, and it can be poured in layers. Each layer should be allowed to set before the next is added, although a slight mixing of layers will again soften the overall effect. The successful use of this method will entail some experiments to gain confidence, and to find the method which produces the effect you required.

One obvious advantage with the plastic resin method is that figures can be shown moving through water by fixing them in position before the resin is poured, and their legs or whatever part of their body is underwater can still be seen. Remember to darken a scale inch or so from the surface of the water of any clothing immersed because the material would soak up the water.

Grass or reeds at the water's edge can be inserted into the resin whilst it is still wet, or holes can be drilled when it is set. The banks are made in the same way as the ground, although you may find it easier to model clumps of earth overhanging or breaking off in plasticene rather than plaster. Fords or beaches are made in the same way, remembering footprints if these would be apparent.

Cliffs and rock faces can be made from cork bark, as used by flower arrangers or model railway modellers. As an alternative to rocks, because, of their weight perhaps, lumps of expanded polystyrene can be broken up to roughly the required shape, and then dipped in a thin mix of Polyfilla to coat them. When these pieces are dry they can be painted to make quite realistic-looking rocks. Careful study of the rock formations found in the area in which the diorama is set, particularly colour photographs in geographical books and magazines (e.g. National Geographic) are very useful when painting a terrain.

What about man-made items such as fences, walls and buildings? There are many ready-made products on sale in model shops which will represent these, or alternatively they can be scratch-built from the usual modelling materials. Wooden fences are perhaps the simplest of all. They can be constructed from balsa or obeche (the harder aircraft modelling wood) rods and dowels, or for untrimmed or prepared logs, twigs from the garden or field. One plant which is particularly good for logs is called Golden Rod, and the dried stems from this are very useful. Fence posts can be made from matchsticks, cocktail sticks or indeed any small pieces of wood. Remember to weather the wood with paint to soften it. Wood exposed to the elements weathers to a grey colour, and a wash of dull grey thinned with turps will run easily over the wood and soak into the grain to give the right effect. Wire is a comparatively modern material for fencing, and fuse wire can be used to give the right effect of sagging or drooping between posts. For barbed wire, there are ready-made varieties now available from model shops, but for the really patient modeller there is nothing quite like the home-made type, with each barb twisted on by hand! If one lacks patience, and if the wire is for small scale figures such as 20 mm, a passable effect can be obtained by tying knots in thin fuse wire or even black thread. Another alternative is to dab adhesive from a tube onto the wire at intervals and sprinkle dried tealeaves over it. With a good paint job the end result is

'Bayonet v Tulwar' – 30 mm setpiece with metal 'Tradition' figures of a British infantryman and a Pathan. The figures are used by the author for North-West frontier skirmish wargames, and show how such figures can be readily displayed as setpieces.

some very nasty-looking, old and rusty barbed wire.

Walls can again be purchased ready-made in plastic, or embossed plastic card can be used. For a really textured finish, the wall can be built up stone by stone, using small pieces of plaster. These are made by pouring a plaster or Polyfilla mix into a greased tin or cardboard box to the depth required for the stones. When it has set, the plaster can be tapped out, broken into the required size pieces, and a wall built using Polyfilla or PVA glue as mortar. Expanded polystyrene can also be used for stone walls, providing it is the very granular type. Emphasize the granules with a soft pencil by drawing around each one to form the stones of the wall. The whole surface can then be given a dark grey wash, remembering to use water-based paint, not enamels because they will eat into the polystyrene and melt it. The thin wash will run into the grooves around the stones, and the rest of the surface can then be painted with a variety of greys or stone colours to match the colour of the kind of stone being represented. Plastered walls can

French Napoleonic light lancer – plastic 'Helmet' figure in a perspex display case by Drumbeat of Cheltenham, showing how effective these cases are.

be made from expanded polystyrene coated with Polyfilla. Cracked plaster and bare patches of the stones or bricks underneath can be made by working on the areas to be left exposed to bring out the stone effect as described, and then plastering around these patches with Polyfilla. Building bricks can be made from lengths of balsa or obeche cut to the right lengths, and again plaster is used as a mortar. Remember to overlap the courses so that the vertical joins do not coincide.

Apart from the odd length of wall, whole buildings can be built up using these methods. There are building kits in card, paper and plastic available, of course, but they are nearly all for the smaller scale figures, up to 25 mm. Britains and Timpo do still make a few buildings which are supposed to be 54 mm scale, but which are in fact grossly undersized and nearer 30 mm. So for the modeller, or wargamer, who want 54 mm scale or larger scale buildings it is a question of scratch-building. The only other possibility are the new snap-together buildings produced by Airfix. These are very good when they have been worked on a little, and carefully painted. Unfortunately, the three buildings available at present cannot be used together because of their widely different styles. The strongpoint or ruin is probably the most useful, as it is a very anonymous style which can be used for a house almost anywhere and anytime from 1500 up to the present day. Simple improvements which can be carried out without much effort include a floor of flagstones or floorboards, internal partitions, a fireplace and hearth, window frames, and beefing up the walls with polystyrene which can then be grained to the same surface as the original outside, or plastered with Polyfilla. The bamboo house is certainly the best model of the series, and only requires painting up to become a very attractive model. It can be used for ancient and modern jungle clashes in South East Asia, and also for incidents in the US wars against the Seminole Indians in the swamps and Everglades of Florida in the 1830s and 1840s.

Ruined buildings are the easiest to make, and a beginner would do well to start with a bombed or burnt-out cottage before tackling anything more ambitious. Beams and rafters are made from balsa or obeche, though if they do not show and are not required to actually hold the structure together they can be omitted. Roof tiles are a little more difficult, because of their shape. If a strip of tiles is made from cardboard or plastic card (soften the latter in hot water to bend it), a plaster mould can be made and tiles cast in latex rubber as required. Slates are much easier, as they can be made just from horizontal strips of the appropriate scale thickness card, cut almost through vertically to make the tiles. The strips are stuck in place starting from the bottom, overlapping each strip so that the edge which still holds the tiles together is hidden beneath the next layer. This is much quicker than laying on each tile individually, and the end result looks exactly the same.

Interiors are often used as settings for dioramas, and these can be most effective. All the methods already described can be used, though usually only three walls of the building or room are constructed. One extra touch which really sets off such a scene is lighting that works! This is not as difficult as it might seem, with the miniature bulbs and holders now available from specialist electronic or radio shops. Lighting must be carefully planned because it is best to avoid burying long runs of wire inside walls or under floorboards; if the wire develops a fault, it will be impossible to replace it without ruining the diorama. The power source can be a small battery hidden behind or underneath the scene, or for larger dioramas a transformer could be fitted so that the mains could be used.

One problem which still remains when the model, its display base, or the diorama are complete is that of protecting it from dust and perhaps prying fingers. A clear cover of some kind is required. If your collection is housed on shelves behind glass doors this is less of a problem, but even then you may like to put one or two special pieces out on display on a desk or table. Clear plastic covers can be purchased from a number of manufacturers, usually those who also sell display bases. These are to set sizes, of course, and so if you have a base or diorama which does not match these sizes you may have to build your own. This can be done from glass, which is quite a difficult operation, or from clear plastic sheet. Even with plastic it takes care and patience to produce a good job, because of the difficulty of making good clean cuts and joins in the sections. Some suppliers of perspex sheet will cut it to size, and this is undoubtedly the best method. The pieces are then glued together with the proper adhesive. As an alternative to do-it-yourself, there are firms which specialize in making clear plastic cases both in specific sizes, and to order for awkward items. Drumbeat of Cheltenham provide this kind of service, and have tackled some difficult problems with figures such as a 77 mm pikeman with his pike extended at an angle of about 45° in front of him!

Wall cabinets with glass shelves, glass sliding doors and top lighting are undoubtedly the best cases in which to display figures. Again there are specialist suppliers, or you can do-it-yourself. A half-way compromise is to use whitewood units, which are built for you but which need finishing by sanding down and varnishing. Veneered chipboard is a cheap material for making cabinets from scratch, but it is robust enough to take the combined weight of glass doors, shelves, and metal soldiers. Carpentry joints are not necessary; the sides, top and bottom are simply butted together and held with the clever little plastic screw jointing blocks now on the market. The glass shelves are also supported on these blocks. Sliding glass doors run in plastic track fitted top and bottom, glued in place with an impact adhesive. The top lighting is fitted using a small fluorescent fitting of the type used under kitchen wall cupboards to illuminate the worktop underneath. If the light does not have a front baffle, a length of softwood beading taken across the width of the top will serve.

9 Finding Out for Yourself

With such a wealth of information on military matters so readily available in the form of books and magazines, one might wonder whether there is any need for a chapter such as this. However, you can be sure that once you begin to become involved in the hobby you will want to do two things; find information, and record it. Wargamers have their own special problems because they are seeking more than uniform details, and I shall not attempt to suggest a solution specifically suited to their needs. For the modeller, his requirements can be defined rather more easily, as they are usually only uniform and equipment details. To begin with, the instructions supplied with a figure, or a book recommended by the maker, will enable the modeller to paint his models. However, if he begins to see them as the basis of a planned collection he will need to find out a little more, perhaps to be able to convert a figure to fill a gap in a regiment's history not available in a commercial range, or to be able to complete a group with a colour bearer and musicians.

The best place to begin to look for more information about the particular subject under consideration is the nearest large reference library. This may mean a trip to a nearby town or city, but simply looking through the index of the military history section will usually provide a list of useful books. Many libraries have special collections which are often of military interest, for example Gloucester City Library has the Birchall American Civil War collection, and Bath City Library has a Napoleon Bonaparte collection. Librarians at reference and local libraries can usually tell you of special collections. Other useful sources of book titles are specialist booksellers' lists which are usually sent out free on application. Publishers' lists are not so useful because they only give the title of books currently in print, and it is the old books long since out of print which are often the most helpful. When you discover what sounds an interesting book, never trust to memory to remember the title. Always write it down, with the fullest possible details, preferably author, full title, number of volumes, whether illustrated, number of pages and size, publisher's name and address, date of publication and price. The index cards in a library are a good guide. This will ensure that you can quote all the details when you are consulting the book again, or are trying to purchase a copy. Specialist booksellers such as Bivouac Books will record your interest in a book or subject and will look for a copy and advise you of anything which might interest you.

There are also specialist military libraries, and these are listed in Appendix 3. Application to consult the books in these libraries must be made in writing, and in some cases special application forms must be completed and referees given.

The various societies listed in Appendix 3 all publish journals, and these are not only useful sources of information in themselves but also review new books and give titles of works used as sources by the authors of articles. Many ordinary, that is non-military, historical societies' journals contain items of military interest. The larger libraries, particularly university libraries, take these journals and usually have copies going back many years. All these publications produce indices, usually to one volume at a time, and articles likely to be of use can be readily identified. There are other unlikely sources of information such as children's comics and advertising posters. In the former category, *Look and Learn* used to have military matters in every issue, often by well-known military experts. In the advertising line, for example, the Post Office produced a poster for its Florence Nightingale stamps showing Crimean uniforms, and Wiggins Teape printed a series of uniform prints by Stadden on various types of their papers as advertising material. The best way to try to keep informed of items like these is to ensure that all your friends or colleagues know of your interest in military history, so that when they find something which you have missed they let you know.

The problem now arises as to how to record and store all this miscellaneous information so that it can be referred to, and the required details found easily and simply. Is it enough to remember that you have the uniform details of the Wurtemberg Telegraph Corps in 1915 somewhere in your library, but not be able to recall quite where? It may be, until you decide to paint up some German World War One figures and want to include a Wurtemberger amongst them. My early efforts were no more than a miscellaneous gathering of folders, loose pages, scraps of card and paper, all in little or no order, and impossible to use easily for reference. Over the few years I have been seriously interested I have evolved a system, and perhaps you can be saved from the problems which beset me by sharing the benefit of my labours.

The object is to make reference easy and, to aid in this, standard components are necessary. The basic component is A4 size lined paper, and this size is maintained throughout. Plain paper will also be needed, and one pad of each of the other A4 paper rulings will be useful. A pocket note-pad, size A5, which can be filed in A4 binders, is useful for carrying around to jot down unexpected finds. However, these are best transferred to A4 paper on returning home. The reason behind the system is that basic information in the form of notes from sources is always on the same size paper. This is in turn stored in, for minor interests, an A4 gusseted wallet. For major interests a hard cover ringbinder is used, which can be subdivided with index guides, using clear plastic enevelopes for plates, photos, cuttings, etc. (for sketches, two different approaches (see p. 49) can be used, assuming that the user is not a natural artist and able to draw the required figures without some form of assistance). Finally, storage for the wallets and binders is required, in the shape of, at its most sophisticated, a filing cabinet or bookcase or, in its simplest form, a plain box of suitable size.

Written descriptions can often be copied verbatim, but the rules of quoting must be followed if any future use of the passage quoted is to be easy. Uniform details are the usual information handled, and a pre-printed pro-forma can help. Whether the information is to be taken from a written description, sketch, or both, a standard approach will be aided by following the headings as set out in Fig. 21. These are spaced down the left hand side of an A4 page, either entered in bulk by hand, or specially printed or typed. The space left for each heading will vary, e.g. 'headgear' does not need as much space as 'coat' but needs more than 'cuffs'. This spacing will depend to a large extent on the periods likely to be covered. For example, for Modern many headings will need no more than one line, simply to act as a reminder in case something odd is worn. The headings ensure that all relevant aspects are covered, and each one should have an entry, even if it is 'not shown' (N/S) in pencil. This can be completed later when known, and avoids any chance of missing an item.

For sketches, a pre-printed outline can be used, Fig. 22. This can be the rather basic approach as shown, or a more elaborate

UNIT RANK		NATIONALITY DATE
HEADGEAR		
COAT COLLAR CUFFS		
EPAULETTES SHOULDER STRAPS		
TROUSERS STRIPE		
GAITERS / LEGGINGS		
BELTS		
EQUIPMENT DEVICES		
BUTTONS BELT PLATES		
KNAPSACK STRAPS		
ROLL STRAPS		
HAVERSACK STRAP		
CANTEEN STRAP / CORD		
SHOES		
RANK DISTINCTIONS		
GENERAL DISTINCTIONS		
SOURCE(S)		

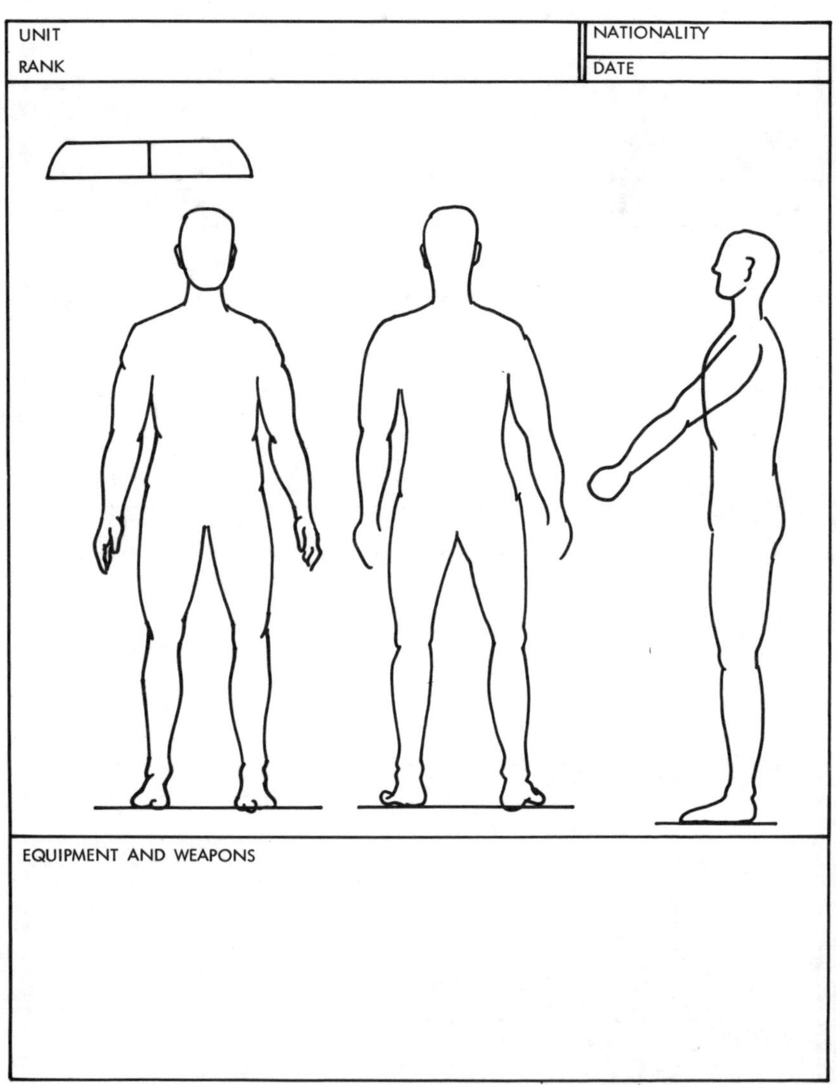
UNIT
NATIONALITY
RANK
DATE
EQUIPMENT AND WEAPONS

one with far more outlines of equipment and other items. In an article in the BMSS bulletin of February 1971, Malcolm Knott ran through all the details of this kind of approach. The lines should be thin, of course, to allow for over-inking the details required. The technique is simple. A blank is taken, and the sketch or photograph copied onto the appropriate outline. Details can be shown to a larger scale on the other outlines, or drawn in the empty areas freehand. It is best to put only one uniform on each form, even though this may mean that some outlines on it are not used. This will allow for further details to be added when they are discovered, and also makes filing very much easier.

An alternative method, which is perhaps simpler and avoids printing costs, is to draw one set of outlines on stout white paper, or tracing paper, and lay a sheet of tracing paper over it. The outline showing through is then used in the same way as the printed blank, and the uniform sketched onto the tracing paper using the outline as a guide. For the actual drawing, a draughtsman's pen such as Rapidograph, with a 0.3 point is recommended. Because of the fine point a very accurate line can be drawn, and small details can be shown without fear of the nib smudging the close lines together. Obviously no attempt at an artistic approach should be aimed for; the sketches are not intended to have any value except for future reference.

Cuttings from newspaper and magazines, etc., photographs and postcards, are best kept in clear plastic envelopes associated with the relevant notes. This allows the material to be referred to without handling and helps to reduce damage. Alternatively, cuttings can be pasted up on plain A4 paper if they are one-sided. A glue stick such as UHU-Stick or Pritt is very useful for this purpose, as the glue is in a neat compact package, easily carried in a briefcase and not at all messy. However, if the cutting is double-sided, or the photo or card has information on the back, the clear envelope is the best answer.

For extracts from books, etc., which are being copied, or notes which are being taken, an order of filing will be needed to allow future reference. For minor interests the loose A4 sheets can be paper-clipped or stapled together for each uniform, i.e. written description and sketch, and stored in a manilla wallet or folder. No subdivision of the wallet is necessary until the contents take considerable sifting to find the item required. Then either a subdivision of the subject in another wallet is necessary, or the entire contents should be transferred to a ringbinder. In the major interests one or more ringbinders are probably best from the start, subdivided as necessary. The order in which the wallets and binders are filed depends to a large extent on the subjects covered. I use a straightforward alphabetical index, e.g. American Civil War, Boer War, French and Indian Wars, etc., with subdivisions such as American Civil War—Union Zouaves, also in alphabetical order. I use this in preference to an historical order, because the system is used by my wife when she helps me, and the alphabetical approach can be followed and used whether one has any knowledge of military history or not.

For articles in magazines or books from which, for any reason, it is not intended to make notes or extracts, a simpler approach which will enable future reference to be made to the relevant article when required will suffice. A separate sheet for each subject can be headed 'Useful References' and the details of any items can then be listed as they are found. Ideally, details should always include the location of the source as well as the title, page number, and coverage, for example where there were illustrations, but simple extracts from indices may suffice.

This may sound like a very elaborate approach to what is basically a very simple problem, but in fact it is not. Deciding on a system and adopting it from the start will save many frustrating hours sifting through books, magazines and loose notes searching for the details you want, and leave you more time to devote to your real interest, the world of military miniatures.

Appendix 1
Makers' Names and Addresses

Details of the larger or more interesting makers of model and toy soldiers are generally available. The number of makers is rapidly increasing, and new firms can be found from advertisements and reviews in the modelling magazines.

Key to abbreviations used

AAC	Aztecs & Conquistadores	MAL	Malburian
ACW	American Civil War	MED	Medieval
AFC	Armoured Fighting Vehicle	MOD	Modern (post-WWII)
ANC	Ancient	MY	Mythical Earth
AR	American Revolution	NAP	Napoleonic
ART	Artillery		(P Peninsular
B	British		W Waterloo)
CAV	Cavalry	NAV	Naval
COL	Colonial	OW	Old West
CR	Crimea	PAS	Pike & Shot
E	Equipment	R	Russian
ECW	English Civil War	SAM	Samurai
F	French	SF	Science Fiction
FP	Franco-Prussian	SYW	Seven Years War
FR	French Revolution	T	Tanks
	(Early Napoleonic)	US	United States
G	German	V	Vehicles
HIST	Historical	W	Weapons
IA	Indian Army	WWI	World War One
INF	Infantry	WWII	World War Two
JR	Jacobite Rebellion		

Action Man

BXL Toy Division, Owen Street, Coalville, Leicester
Roughly 1/6 scale plastic jointed figures, with material clothes, plastic weapons and equipment. Range includes MOD, NAV, WWII. Although designed as toys, these figures can be used as

display pieces, particularly the weapons range. Colour catalogue (Palitoy, trade). Toy shops.

Airfix Products Ltd
*Haldane Place, Garratt Lane, London SW*18
Makers of HO/00 and 1/32 scale polythene and polystyrene figures, buildings, vehicles and equipment. Assembled and kit form, suitable for beginners and experts. Quality from poor to excellent (many of the poorer figures being remade to higher standard). Illustrated colour catalogues. Toy and hobby/model shops.

Almirall
see MODEL and HOBBY (Appendix 2)

Armtec
see MICRO-MOLD (Appendix 1)

Bellona
see MICRO-MOLD (Appendix 1)

Brigadier
see MODEL and HOBBY (Appendix 2)

Britains Ltd
*Blackhorse Lane, London E*17
Standard scale (small 54 mm) plastic figures.

C-in-C
see MICRO-MOLD (Appendix 1)

Ciuffo, John
see SEAGULL MODEL (GB) LTD (Appendix 2)

Elastolin
O. & M. Hausser, 8632 *Neustadt Bei Coburg, Postfach* 1260, *Eisfelder Strasse* 17, *West Germany*
70 mm and 40 mm hand-painted hard plastic figures, well animated, highly detailed. ANC, ART, MED, OW. Illustrated colour catalogues. UK agent: D. Hawkins, The Studio, Shortands, 568 Mumbles Road, Oystermouth, Swansea, Glam.

Flat Figures
see MODEL AND HOBBY (Appendix 2)

Frontier
see MODEL FIGURES AND HOBBIES (Appendix 2)

Greenwood and Ball Ltd
61 *Westbury Street, Thornaby-on-Tees, Tees-side*
Sanderson, Lasset, Cameo, Greenwood & Ball metal 54 mm figures, very high quality, mainly fully assembled, animated in a wide variety of poses, and primed. ANC, AR, COL, ECW, FR, MED, NAP, WWII. Garrison 25 mm metal wargames figures, highly detailed, excellent quality. ANC, ECW, NAP, SYW. Designed by John Braithewaite. The SYW range particularly good, should do much to popularize this most interesting period. Illustrated catalogues. Uniform cards. Mail order and model shops.

Helmet Products
Betchworth, Surrey
54 mm PVA plastic kits, CR, NAP. Inexpensive range, foot and mounted, designed for simple assembly and mass display. Lists. Colour illustration with each kit. Mail order and model/hobby shops.

Heriocs Figures
22 *Mowbray Court, Mowbray Road, London SE*19 2*RL*
1/300 metal ACW, ANC, NAP, WWII figures, artillery, vehicles, tanks. Excellent detail, especially NAP range, worthy of HO/OO scale figures—indeed better than some. Lists. Mail order and model/hobby shops.

Hinchliffe Models Ltd
*Meltham, Huddersfield HD*7 3*NX*
75 mm, 54 mm, 25 mm, 20 mm metal figures. Illustrated catalogue.

Hinton Hunt Figures Marketing Ltd
*River Road, Taplow, Maidenhead, Berks SL*6 *OBE*
54 mm and 20 mm metal figures, various periods, ready assembled, solid and chunky style. Catalogues. Mail order, model shops. Own shop; Military Heritage, 27 Camden Passage, Antique Village, Islington, London.

Historex
Historex Agents, 3 *Castle Street Dover, Kent C*16 1*QJ*
54 mm polystyrene AR, HIS, NAP figures. Foot, mounted, artillery, field forge, equipment, all in kit form. Superb quality, super detailed, not for beginners. Comprehensive parts list (over 300 separate items). 1/35 WWII polystyrene figures, weapons and

equipment. Oil-bound poster paints, sable brushes, tools, pyrogravure, display cases (plastic and glass) and bases, uniform prints (NAP), books, Hinchliffe 75 mm metal figures (kits). Illustrated colour and black/white catalogues (includes valuable painting and modelling information). Mail order and model shops.

Imrie/Risley Miniatures
Copiague, New York 11726, *USA*
54 mm and 1/24 scale metal unassembled figures. Most periods, excellent quality. Especially good on US Army and in particular all the armies in the American Revolution, in a wide variety of poses. Illustrated catalogue. Full painting guide (mainly in colour) with all figures. Own range matt paints, palettes, brushes, display bases, epoxy glue, reference books and uniform cards. Mail order and model/hobby shops. UK agent; Under Two Flags, 4 St Christophers Place, Wigmore, London W1.

JAC Castings
46 *Rowlands Road, Greenfield Farm, Horsham, Sussex* (*Horsham* 66241)
70 mm 'System 70' metal castings, assembled and primed, B. COL. Nicely detailed and interestingly posed figures. 54 mm metal foot and mounted figures, as kits, or assembled and primed. ECW, MED. Interesting and unusual range. Lists. Mail order.

Jackboot
see MODEL FIGURES AND HOBBIES
SEAGULL MODEL (GB) LTD (Appendix 2)

K & L Company
PO Box 3781, *Tulsa, Oklahoma* 74152, *USA*
Metal ACW IIO (20 mm) (3.5 mm) unpainted figures and equipment. Extensive (over 80 figures) range infantry, cavalry, artillery. High quality, well detailed. Includes Zouaves, also civilians, musicians. Also civilians (period). Illustrated list. Prices c 18–25 INF; c 50–60 CAV; c 20–$1.35 ART. 'Hardtack' ACW wargame rules. Antique ACW minie-balls.

Laing, Peter
11 *Bounds Oak Way, Southborough, Tunbridge Wells, Kent TN4 OUB*
15 mm metal figures 1066, ANC, COL, CR, ECW, MAL, WWI. Scale is 1/20; 2½ mm: 1 ft. Supplied as cast, but amount of flash

is small and can be easily cleaned with knife or file. Detail is good, and super-detail such as reins, bayonets, etc., can be easily added with fuse wire and pins. Extensive range of equipment, artillery, etc., available. New figures being added continually. Excellent for wargames and dioramas. Lists. Wargames rules.

Lamming Miniatures
45 *Wenlock Street, Hull HU*3 1*DA* (*Hull* 26896)
25 mm metal figures ANC, NAP, MED. Catalogue.

Lippett Figures
46 *The Old High Street, Folkestone, Kent CT*20 1*RN* (*Folkestone* 58676)
90 mm metal figures MED (100 Years War) foot and mounted figures, and ART. Lists.

Miniature Figurines
28/32 *Northam Road, Southampton, Hants SO*2 *ONZ*
High quality, well detailed unpainted castings. (Scale is 5 mm : 1 ft.) 25 mm metal figures, ACW, ANC, AR, ECW, MAL, MED, MY, NAP, OW, PAS, SAM, SF, SYW. The largest range of 25 mm scale figures available, very high quality, mostly designed by Dick Higgs, a vast and comprehensive coverage of the armies of the major periods (and many of the minor ones), constantly being redesigned and remade to even higher standards! Excellent for wargames, dioramas or displays. 15 mm metal figures ANC, ECW, NAP. Nicely detailed castings, cast in multiples on strips, good for dioramas. 5 mm metal castings, Horse and Musket, cast in blocks ART, CAV, INF WWII; Warships, ACW, ANC, NAP, WWI. Paints, books, wargames rules. Illustrated catalogue, with uniform, etc. articles. Mail order and model/hobby shops. US: Miniature Figurines USA Inc, 4311 Lemmon Avenue, Dallas, Texas 75219, USA.

Men o' War
52 *Blenheim Drive, Welling, Kent DA*16 3*LY*
99 mm metal figures, in kit or assembled. Small range of various periods, continual new additions. The Royal Artillery Drum Major 1840–7 is a small masterpiece. Illustrated catalogue. B/W photo and uniform details with each figure. Mail order and model/ hobby shops.

Micro-Mold
1–2 *Unifax, Woods Way, Goring-by-Sea, Sussex*
20 mm C-in-C metal castings, ACW, AR, NAP. Finely detailed, especially ART pieces, unpainted. 1/285 C-in-C metal WWII AFVs, ART, excellent detail, revolving turrets, in-scale barrels, unpainted. 1/200 Mercator AFVs; MOD, WWI, WWII, painted high quality castings. Bellona plastic wargame and diorama pieces. Particularly useful to the model soldier collector are the five sizes of diorama trays, and eight different model stands (in two sets), all moulded in white plastic. 1/35, 1/48, 1/72 Armtec WWII parts and accessories, plastic. Books, wargames rules, military prints. Catalogues (illustrated) and lists. Mail order.

Nostalgia Models
S. Wade 37, *David Road, Acton, London W*3
Unusual toy soldier-type figures in the Britains style, available painted in gloss colours, of the more interesting and unusual units of the British Empire. These will appeal particularly to Britains collectors.

Old Guard, The
New Hope Design, Rothbury, Sunderland
54 mm metal kit-form figures (no. of pieces varies), ACW, ANC, AR, NAP, SAM, SYW, WWI, G COL, unpainted. Very high-quality castings, many unusual figures, e.g. ANC includes Roman catapult and crew, WWII includes Stuart tanks and crew! New figures regularly added. 54 mm metal Deauville F NAP figures, again refreshingly different, e.g. off-duty poses. 1/24 scale metal AR, HIST, Red Indians, well-animated and detailed figures in a larger scale, excellent quality. Illustrated list. Campaign paints. Mail order and model/hobby shops. US agent: 33 North Main Street, New Hope, Pennsylvania 18938, USA.

Phoenix Model Developments Ltd
*The Square, Earls Barton, Northampton NN*6 *ONA*
54 mm, 30 mm, 25/20 mm metal figures. Catalogue. Mail order and model/hobby shops.

Rollo
see MODEL and HOBBY (Appendix 2)

Rose Miniatures
Russell Gamage MSIA, 15 *Llanover Road, London SE*18 3*ST*
54 mm metal figures, 1880–1914 B, G, I, R; AR, ART, ANC, Aztecs, COL, MED, MOD, NAP, NAV, PAS, WWI, WWII, multi-piece castings, good quality, rather delicate appearance, painted and unpainted. 54 mm Elite metal figures, superior detailed multi-piece castings. 25 mm and 30 mm wargames figures, ACW, ANC, AR, ART, COL, ECW, NAP, WWI. Paints, brushes, uniform prints, metal strip and sheet for reins, *shabraques*, etc. Extensive parts list, e.g. heads, arms, weapons; 54 mm only. Catalogue, illustrated in colour and B/W.

Scruby, Jack
6744 *Avenue* 304, *Goshen, California* 93227
Metal castings in 90 mm, 75 mm, 30 mm, 25 mm, 20 mm, and N-gauge. ACW, ANC, AR, COL, FP, MED, Mexican 1847, NAP, NAV, PAS, SYW. Full-round, three dimensional, cast of the finest tin-lead (solder) alloy, can be bent without breaking (ideal for conversion or animation). Ranges constantly being redesigned and updated. Wargames scale figures are not intended as collectors' items, being designed for wargames and to withstand rough handling. Collectors' sizes include some unusual pieces. Special 45 mm Napoleonic Peninsular range include British rifle brigade, French light infantry, Spanish guerillas, based on C. S. Forester's book *Death to the French*, designed for 1 : 1 wargames using Skirmish Wargames Napoleonic Rules (see Appendix 6). Rule books, magazine. Mail order only in UK.

S.E.G.O.M.
*Model Figures & Hobbies, Lower Balloo Road, Groomsport, Bangor, Co Down BT*19 2*LU*
54 mm plastic (cellulose acetate) figures. AR, NAP, PAS(B), SYW(F), WWI(F), WWII(G), Personalities, all in kit form. B/W picture and colouring details with each figure. List. 54 mm plastic (cellulose acetate) spare parts, over 270 different pieces, e.g. heads, arms, bodies, legs, weapons, etc. Illustrated catalogue. Simple but well detailed kits, easy to assemble and convert, and when painted good display pieces. 30 mm (small, actually nearer 25 mm) cellulose acetate plastic wargames figures NAP only, B, F, G, R. Figures one piece, some cavalry have alternative arms to allow variations (e.g. officers), horses in two halves. Poses rather inactive

for wargaming, e.g. stood still, but good detail. List. Booklet on converting, etc. *How To Animate (SEGOM) Miniatures.*

Sentry Box, The
F/T./LT/Mrs P. J. Edmonds, 28 *Carters Way, Wisborough Green, Billingshurst, Sussex* (*Wisborough Green* 623)
12 cm metal figures (scale 20 mm : 1 ft, figures approx 5 in. high). Mainly full ceremonial dress of British army from early twentieth century to WWII, painted, or unpainted and unassembled. 54 mm metal figures, historical, e.g. Henry VIII and wives, painted or unpainted. Catalogue. Colour photographs available separately. Epoxy metal putty, Plaka paint, perspex cases. Mail order only.

Series 77
25, *Britannia Drive, Gravesend, Kent DA*12 4*RP*
77 mm metal figures ANC, B CAV 1790–1815, CAN 1885, ECW, NAP, PAS, WWII pilots, foot and mounted, painted or unpainted and primed. High quality castings. Colouring guide with each figure. List. Mail order and model/hobby shops.

Spencer-Smith Miniatures
Ronald W. Spencer-Smith, 66 *Longmeadow, Frimley, Camberley* (*Camberley* 21618)
30 mm plastic Standard range wargames figures, ACW, AR, MOD, NAP, unpainted. 30 mm plastic Connoisseur range wargames figures, AR, NAP, unpainted; much greater detail, suitable for dioramas, etc. Lists.

Tradition
188 *Piccadilly, London W*1*V* 9*DA* (01–734–1352/3/4)
120 mm metal Cameron figures, COL, NAP, painted and unpainted. 90 mm metal Stadden figures, B 1900, B MOD, NAP, kits, painted and unpainted. 75 mm metal Reynard figures, knights. 54 mm metal Stadden figures, ACW, ANC, AR, COL, CR, ECW, FP, HIST, JR, MAL, MED, MOD, NAP, NAV, SAM, SYW, WWI, WWII, assembled, painted or unpainted. Various positions can be requested at extra cost. Book of colour photographs, entitled *Model Soldiers*. 54 mm Hinton Hunt figures. 30 mm metal Stadden figures, AR, B and G 1890–1914, COL, CR, IA, MED, NAP, SYW, WWI, WWII, high quality, well detailed and animated castings, unpainted only. 25 mm

metal Tradition figures, 1066, ACW, ANC, AR, CR, FP, JR, MAL, NAP, SAM, SYW, WWI, unpainted. Lists. Militaria, accessories, old metal figures (Britains, etc.) Mail order and shop.

Trophy Miniatures
131 *Plassey Street, Penarth, Glam.*
54 mm metal figures in knockdown kit form, foot and mounted. Single figures from numerous periods, good detail. List.

21st Century Antiques Ltd
PO Box No. 14; *Crawley, Sussex RH*11 7*RW*
105 mm Great Men of War series metal busts.

Warrior Metal Miniatures
23 *Grove Road, Leighton Buzzard, Beds LY*7 8*SF*
25 mm metal figures, 1066, ANC, ECW, NAP, PAS, nicely detailed castings, including NAP gun crews for foot and horse ART for all main protagonists, and Irregular castings useful for seventeenth century to ACW! List. Wargame rules. Mail order and model/hobby shops.

Willie Figures
Ed Suren, 60 *Lower Sloane Street, London SW*1 (01-730-7615)
30 mm metal figures, foot and mounted, 1066, 1750, ANC, ART, COL, CR, FR, NAP, PAS, well-detailed and highly animated figures, painted or unpainted. Excellent for dioramas. 60 mm camp followers—partially in uniform! CR, NAP, painted or unpainted. List. Mail order and shop. Militaria.

Appendix 2
Specialist Suppliers

A list of sources for books, specialist equipment, tools, modelling accessories and spare parts.

Bivouac Books Ltd
104 *Kilburn Square, London NW*6 6*PS*
Specialists in military books for all periods, both new and second-hand. Special lists for subjects and periods. Lists sent out regularly and particular requirements and interests noted for reference if details sent to them. Run by Pat Quorn, the retail premises are well worth visiting if only for the experience of meeting him, never mind the large quantities of books always in stock which include many bargains.

BMW (Models)
327-329 *Haydons Road, Wimbledon, London SW*19 8*LB*
Large stockists of wargames and collectors' figures, paints, tools and accessories by many makers. Personal and mail order. Numerous lists and catalogues available.

Drumbeat Showcases
J. W. Davis & V. M. Davis, 31 *Stamford Mill Road, Cheltenham, Glos GL*53 7*QH* (*Cheltenham* 36519)
Perspex display cases with wooden bases, excellent quality. Dust covers for single figures and small groups, and sliding front cabinets for larger displays. Dust covers in six sizes, cabinets in four. Also made-to-measure service for special requirements. Mail order. Sets of replica Victorian nursery soldiers, perspex, hand painted. List.

Hamleys of Regent Street
200-202 *Regent Street, London W*1*R* 5*DF* (01-734-3161)
Large toy shop, stockists of many figure ranges.

HR Products Inc
9232 *Waukegan Road, Morton Grove, Illinois* 60053, *USA*
54 mm metal weapons, equipment, artillery and some figures, numerous periods. 1 in. : 1 ft. scale metal weapons. HO tanks and artillery. Fine detail, weapons, etc., excellent for conversions, etc.

List. UK agent: I. R. F. Thompson, 54 Uplands Road, South Croydon, Surrey CR2 6RE. Mail order only.

A. A. Johnston
Military Books and Prints, Pitney, Langport, Som.
All manner of military books stocked, new and secondhand, including a large range of imported titles, especially catering for the model soldier enthusiast. Specific titles obtained if not in stock. A first class service, at sensible prices. Official distributors for Imrie/Risley plates, DO Enterprises (*Militaria Magazine*), Military Arms Research Service, Military Collectors Service, Hourtelle plates, Le Plumel plates, and Knotel Uniformenkunde plates. Regular lists sent out by genial Arthur Johnston, himself a model soldier collector and BMSS member.

Mainly Military
103 *Walsall Road, Lichfield, Staffs*
Mail order suppliers of collectors and wargames figures, accessories, etc., fast, efficient and friendly, run by collectors and wargamers. Series 77, H Hunt, Lasset, Rose, Soldat, Miniature Figurines, Greening card AFVs, Leicester Micro Tanks. 54 mm parts and accessories (Lasset, Rose, Mini Figs) ideal for conversions. Wooden display bases, display cases, painting instructions, Plaka paints, books, uniform prints (Tambour, Knotel, PJH, Chevron, Le Plumet, K/S). Painting service. Regular lists.

Model and Hobby
Frederiksborggade 23, 1360 *Copenhagen K Denmark*
54 mm figures and components: Rollo, Rose, HR, Almirall, Historex, H Hunt, and others (metal and plastic), all periods. 50 mm metal Brigadier wargames figures and components (almost toy soldiers in appearance). 30 mm metal flat figures, unpainted: Sima, Herbu, Hafer, Ochel, Scholtz, Tobinnus, Volrath, Sivhed and others, over 150,000 different figures, all periods, all countries. 20 mm plastic figures (Airfix) and buildings (Heljan). Uniform plates, books, military postcards, both new and old. Modelling and hobby materials. Catalogues. Mail order and shop.

Model Figures and Hobbies
*Lower Balloo Road, Groomsport, Co Down BT*19 2*LU* (*Groomsport* 387)
SEGOM 54 mm and 30 mm plastic figures (see App. 1). Jackboot 54 mm metal figures, kits or assembled and primed, all figures

with painting instructions, MOD(B), WWI(G), WWII (G). Kits must be assembled and animated, and so are not for beginners. Good detail. Weapon and equipment spares. Frontier 54 mm metal figures, assembled and animated. Range covers all periods, with interesting and unusual figures. Quality of B range shows much improvement on A range, but these are inexpensive metal figures and paint up nicely. Additional animation if required. Figures also made to special order. Rose, Greenwood & Ball, Stadden and other UK makers. HR 54 mm weapons and equipment. Display and posting boxes, heavy black plastic display bases. Lists. Mail order specialists.

Moulds—Ready Made
K. & G. Marketing Ltd, 8 *Front Street, Cullercoats, N. Shields, Northumberland*
Rubber moulds and casting accessories, available through local stockists such as toy or hobby shops. Mail order for eighteenth-century figure moulds; Westby Products, East Keswick, Leeds LS17 9EH.

Norths Uniform Cards
John Edgcombe, Flat A, 6 *Willow Road, London NW*3 1*TH*
Useful series of paint-your-own uniform cards covering Napoleonic and 1900-14 periods. Also uniform charts, and 30 mm cut-out card figures. SAE for all details.

Precision Petite Ltd
119*a High Street, Teddington, Middx TW*11 8*HG* (01–977–0878)
Power drill, battery or transformer driven, with specialist bits, stand, flexible drive, etc. Useful tool for the dedicated modeller who wants to speed up such processes as cleaning up castings, drilling holes for lances, engraving name plates etc. SAE for illustrated leaflets.

Scale Drawings
F. Howard, 17 *Trevor Road, Southport, Lancs PR*8 3*PJ*
Fully dimensional constructional drawings of British muzzle loading artillery and ancillary vehicles. Very useful for scratch builders.

Seagull Model (GB) Ltd
15 *Exhibition Road, London SW*7 (01–584–2758)
Stockists of figures, card models and buildings, plastic AFV and

maritime kits, tools and accessories. Makes include Lasset, Jackboot, JAC, Kirk, Phoenix, Airfix, SEGOM, Tamiya, Bandai, Series 77, Men O'War, Aurora, Eidai, Fujimi, Hasegawa, Monogram, Midori, Italaerei, Esci. Valda 54 mm metal kits, with painting instructions, unusual subjects, e.g. Women's services WWI. Valiant and Merite 54 mm metal kits, with painting instructions, US manufactures, excellent quality figures of unusual subjects, e.g. gunfighters. Catalogue (illustrated). Paints – Humbrol, Testors, Campaign. Sable paint brushes. Mail order and shop. Painting service for figures to special order. Figures and dioramas by John Ciuffo in plasticene. These are real works of art, and can be specially commissioned.

Spare Parts, Weapons and Accessories

This is a list of the spare parts, weapons and accessories available for use in conversions and scratch building. The scale is shown in the first column (e.g. 77 mm), the material is shown in the second column (e.g. plastic or metal) and the maker's and/or supplier's name, as listed in Appendix 1 or 2, is shown in the third column (e.g. HR Products).

77 mm		**Series 77**
54 mm	Metal	**Miniature Figurines**
		Mainly Military
		HR Products
		Lasset (Greenwood & Ball)
		Hinton Hunt
		Jackboot (Model Figures & Hobbies)
		Phoenix
	Plastic	**Historex**
		Segom (Model Figures & Hobbies)
1/35th	Plastic	**Armtec**
30 mm	Metal	**Brigadier (Model & Hobbies)**
	Plastic	**Armtec**
25 mm	Metal	**Miniature Figurines**
1/72nd	Plastic	**Armtec**

Strand Glass Co Ltd

Brentway Trading Estate, Brentford, Middx (01–568–7191)

Mould making and resin casting materials, including vinamold, silicone, rubber, clear resin, polyurethane foam, latex rubber, plaster, epoxy resin, modelling putty, polyurethane sheets, release agents etc. Illustrated lists (relevant materials are given at the back of the glass fibre catalogue). Mail order service, and retail shops in fifteen large towns.

Tiranti, Alex, Ltd
72 Charlotte Street, London W1
Silastic cold-cure silicone rubber.

Appendix 3
Specialist Societies and Libraries

British Model Soldier Society
Secretary: John Ruddle, 22 Priory Gardens, Hampton, Middx TW12 29Z. Membership is a must for the serious collector or modeller. Meetings are held in London on the last Friday in each month at the Caxton Hall, and all of the growing number of provincial branches throughout the country hold meetings regularly. All types of modellers and collectors are welcomed, and all kinds of figures, connoisseur and toy, metal and plastic. The society provides displays for many of the hobby shows and has a permanent display of models from the BMSS National Collection on exhibition at Dodington House, near Bath in Somerset.

The quarterly bulletin contains articles contributed by members on model soldiers, modelling, collecting, uniforms and all aspects of the hobby, and is illustrated with drawings and photographs.

British Museum Reading Room
Director's Office (Reader's Tickets), The British Museum, London WC1B 3DG
A priceless collection of military history books, many unobtainable elsewhere. Admission by reader's ticket only, which must be obtained in advance from the address above.

International Plastic Modellers' Society
Secretary: J. W. Salmon, Oakbank, 35 Clares Green Road, Spencers Wood, Reading RG7 1DY.
For all aspects of plastic modelling, including military modelling. Publishes bi-monthly magazine. Regular meetings held, branches throughout the UK and overseas. Membership of great value to those who enjoy modelling plastic kits, whether beginners or experts.

Miniature Armoured Fighting Vehicles Society
Secretary British Branch: D. Rodgers, 57 Carlton Road, Birkenhead, Cheshire
Editor: G. L. Dooley, 2 Meddowcroft Road, Wallasey, Cheshire L45 UR
For the AFV modeller rather than the model soldier enthusiast, but articles on modern uniforms are often included. Publishes journal, *Tankette.*

National Army Museum Reading Room
The Director, National Army Museum, Royal Hospital Road, Chelsea, London SW3 4HT
Research facilities are available to holders of reader's tickets which may be obtained on written application. The library contains about 20 000 books on the British Army including a full range of regimental histories and army lists, campaign histories, military biographies, drill books and pamphlets, current historical and regimental journals, and archives containing letters, journals and papers of many important military figures. In addition there are print and drawing, and photographic collections.

Public Records Office
Chancery Lane, London WC2
Contains many millions of documents relating to the actions of central government and the courts of law of England and Wales from the eleventh century, including many original documents of military interest, e.g. reports by commanders in the field, etc. Admission by reader's ticket only, obtainable from the address given.

Regimental Museums
Many regimental museums have research facilities available to serious students of military history, and of course a trip around such a museum can often provide the answer to a problem over dress or equipment. An excellent guide to regimental museums in Great Britain is available from Bellona/Micro Mold.

Scottish Military Collectors' Society
Editor: J. Yule, 33 Evelyn Terrace, Perth PH2 OBS
For those interested in Scottish regular, militia and yeomanry uniforms and badges, etc. Regular journal *Despatch.*

Society for Army Historical Research
Hon. Secretary: c/o The Library, Old War Office, Whitehall, London SW1
For those interested in the British Army and the land forces of the Empire, embracing both army and regimental history, military antiques, dress, arms and equipment, customs and traditions, and the history of the art of war. Publishes a quarterly journal which contains articles on all these topics.

Society of Ancients
Secretary: J. Norris, Hillside, Jacksons Lane, London N6 5SR
Mainly a wargames society; regular journal *Slingshot* contains articles on uniforms, equipment, weapons, etc.

Society of Friends of the National Army Museum
The Director, National Army Museum, Royal Hospital Road, London SW3 4HT
The income of the society is used to buy important relics and research material for the NAM which might otherwise be lost to the nation. An annual reception and private visits to special exhibitions are arranged for members, and the Museum's annual report is received free of charge. In addition, members' requests for assistance with military research problems are given priority (see NAM Reading Room). If you care for the history and traditions of the British Army, and the old Indian Army, please become a Friend.

War Office Library
Old War Office Building, Whitehall, London
An extensive library of books and journals on all areas of military history, in particular the British Army. Book lists of the periods and subjects are published, and an index to these is also available.

Appendix 4
Magazines

Airfix Magazine
Editor: Bruce Quarie, Bar Hill, Cambridge CB3 8EL
Covers all aspects of plastic modelling, often contains useful information on military subjects. Reviews new figures and kits, etc.

Armies and Weapons
Interconair, 1 Camp Road, Farnborough, Hants GU14 6EN
English translation of an Italian magazine which covers mainly modern or WWII subjects, especially AFVs, but contains the odd article on other periods. Well illustrated with black-and-white photos, some colour artwork.

Battle
Editor: as 'Military Modelling'.
Covers all aspects of military history, with special emphasis on modern developments, to complement ' Military Modelling'.

Military Modelling
Editor: Alec Gee, MAP, PO Box 35, Bridge Street, Hemel Hempstead, Herts HP1 1EE
Devoted entirely to all aspects of military modelling, contains articles on wargames, painting, converting, military history. Comprehensive reviews of new books, kits, figures, etc. Reports on specialist society activities and events. Essential reading in order to keep up with new products, ideas, etc.

Miniature Warfare and Model Soldiers
Formstan Ltd, Stanhope House, Fairbridge Road, London N19 3HZ
Mainly for wargamers, but occasionally contains articles on collecting and uniforms.

Savage and Soldier
Editor: Doug Johnson, c/o 1 Cohen 9797 Litzinger Road, St. Louis, Missouri 63124 USA

Aimed mainly at wargamers, this delightful little magazine will be of interest to anyone interested in the Colonial armies and wars.

Soldier
Editor: P. N. Wood, Clayton Barracks, Aldershot, Hants GU11 2BG
Covers the activities of the modern British Army, with occasional historical articles. Reviews books, figures, records, etc.

Sword and Lance
Editors: A. S. Watson and G. J. North, 38, Coniscliffe Road, Darlington, Co. Durham
Covers all aspects of military history, modelling, etc.

Tradition
Editor: Lt Col J. B. R. Nicholson, 188 Piccadilly, London W1V 9DA
Journal of the International Society of Military Collectors, this is a high-quality, beautifully produced glossy with colour artwork for the cover and centre plates. Articles on all aspects of military history, weapons, uniforms, etc. Reviews of books, and sometimes figures.

Wargamers Newsletter
Editor: Don Featherstone; Editorial: 69 Hill Lane, Southampton, Hants SO1 5AD. Subs and queries: c/o Tradition, 188 Piccadilly, London W1V 9DA.
Although aimed primarily at wargamers, this lively magazine covers also uniforms, etc., of interest to the collector. Good reviews of new products, figures, books and rules, etc.

Appendix 5
Further Reading

Model and Toy Soldiers

DILLEY, R., *Scale Model Soldiers*, Almark, 1972.

FEATHERSTONE, D., *Handbook for Model Soldier Collectors*, Kaye & Ward, 1969.

FEATHERSTONE, D., *Military Modelling*, Kaye & Ward, 1970.

GARRATT, J. G., *Model Soldiers; a Collectors Guide*, Seeley Service, London.

GARRATT, J. G., *Model Soldiers for the Connoisseur*, Weidenfeld & Nicholson, 1973.

HARRIS, H., *Model Soldiers*, Weidenfeld & Nicholson.

RICHARDS, L., *Old British Model Soldiers* 1895–1918, Arms & Armour, 1970.

Ancient to Modern Periods

BARKER, P., *Armies of the Macedonian & Punic Wars*, Wargames Research Group, 1971.

BARKER, P., *Armies & Enemies of Imperial Rome* 150 *B.C.*–600 *A.D.*, Wargames Research Group, 1971.

SAXTORPH, N. M., *Warriors & Weapons of Early Times* 3000 *B.C.*–1700 *A.D.*, Blandford Press, 1972.

FIRTH, C., *Cromwell's Army* (University paperback), Methuen.

YOUNG, P., *Edgehill*, Roundwood, 1967.

NORMAN, A. V. R., AND POTTINGER, D., *Warrior to Soldier* 449–1600, Weidenfeld & Nicholson, 1966.

DUFFY, C., *The Army of Frederick the Great*, David & Charles, 1974.

KATCHER, P., *American Provincial Corps* 1775–1784, Osprey, 1973.

LEFFERTS, C., *Uniforms in the American Revolution*, WE, Inc., Connecticut.

FUNKEN, L. AND F., *Uniforms & Weapons of the First Empire* (2 vols.), Casterman, 1973.

NORTH, R., *Regiments at Waterloo*, Almark, 1971.
NORTH, R., *Soldiers of the Peninsular War*, Almark, 1972.
PERICOLI, U., *The Armies at Waterloo*, Seeley Service, 1973.
WINDROW, M., AND EMBLETON, G., *Military Dress of the Peninsular War*, Ian Allen, 1974.

BLAKE, M., *American Civil War Cavalry*, Almark, 1970.
BLAKE, M., *American Civil War Infantry*, Almark, 1973.
CHATER, C. P., *An Assemblage of Indian Army Soldiers and Uniforms*, Perpetua Press, 1973.

FUNKEN, L. AND F., *Uniforms & Weapons of the First World War* (2 vols.), Casterman, 1974.
NASH, D., *German Infantry* 1914–1918, Almark, 1970.
NASH, D., *German Artillery* 1914–1918, Almark, 1971.

DILLEY, R., *US Army Uniforms* 1939–1945, Almark, 1972.
DILLEY, R., *Japanese Army Uniforms & Equipment* 1939–1945, Almark, 1970.
FUNKEN, L. AND F., *Uniforms & Weapons of the Second World War* (2 vols.), Casterman, 1974.

General

ANDRESS, M., *'N' Gauge Model Railways*, Almark, 1972.
AHERN, J. H., *Miniature Landscape Modelling*, MAP, 1970.
BOWLING, A. H., *Scottish Regiments* 1660–1914, Almark, 1971.
BOWLING, A. H., *British Regiments* 1660–1914, Almark, 1970.
FUNKEN, L. AND F., *Uniforms & Weapons of the Soldiers of All Times*, Casterman, 1974.
KANNICK, P., *Military Uniforms of the World*, Blandford, 1968.
LAWSON, C. C. P., *History of the Uniforms of the British Army* (5 vols.), Kaye & Ward.
NORTH, R., *Military Uniforms* 1686–1918, Hamlyn, 1970.
WILKINSON-LATHAM, R. AND C., *Infantry Uniforms Britain & Commonwealth* (2 vols.), Blandford, 1969.
WILKINSON-LATHAM, R. AND C., *Cavalry Uniforms Britain & Commonwealth*, Blandford, 1969.
WINDROW, M., *French Foreign Legion*, Osprey, 1971.
WINDROW, M., AND EMBLETON, G., *Military Dress in North America* 1665–1970, Military Book Society, 1973.

Appendix 6
Wargames

Wargaming is a fascinating hobby in its own right, but it is often first discovered through an initial interest in the model soldiers themselves without any thought of putting them to use. There are a number of books available which will introduce the hobby to the newcomer, and take him on to the more advanced levels if the game really interests him. The nearest thing to an official journal of the hobby, the *Wargamers Newsletter*, has already been mentioned, and its editor, Don Featherstone, has written most of the readily available books on wargaming as well as a number of excellent military history books. A full list is available from the author at 69 Hill Lane, Southampton, SO1, 5AD, England. Don Featherstone also has various sets of rules for the main wargaming periods available, mainly aimed at the beginner.

Modellers interested in using the larger scale, e.g. 54 mm figures for wargaming are catered for specifically by Skirmish Wargames, 13 St Decumans Road, Watchet, Somerset, TA23 OHR, England, who produce rule books which also contain historical details, modelling and conversion ideas and a wealth of background information for the periods concerned. A SAE will bring full details. Although these handbooks are specially intended for the larger figures, games can be played using the more usual wargames scales, e.g., 25 mm.

Many other sets of rules and books on the subject are advertised in the specialist magazines listed in Appendix 4. In addition most towns, and even schools, have wargames clubs, and the address of your local society should be obtainable from hobby shops, the main public library, or the local authority information officer. By the time this book is published, *Military Modelling* magazine should have published a national directory of wargames and model soldier clubs, obtainable from the magazine.